HEREIN LIES THE TREASURE-TROVE

– volume one –

Instructional Talks of Tripitaka Master Hua

Translated into English by
Dharma Realm Buddhist University
International Institute For The
Translation of Buddhist Texts

Talmage, California

1983

HEREIN LIES THE TREASURE-TROVE, VOLUME I

Reviewed By: Bhikshuni Heng Tao, Bhikshuni Heng Hsien
Edited By: Bhikshuni Heng Ch'ih, Bhikshuni Heng Liang, Bhikshuni Heng Chia, and Susan Rounds

Certified By: Venerable Abbot Hua, Bhikshuni Heng Ch'ih, Bhikshuni Heng Tao

COPYRIGHT © 1983 BY THE SINO-AMERICAN BUDDHIST ASSOCIATION, DHARMA REALM BUDDHIST UNIVERSITY

PRINTED IN THE UNITED STATES OF AMERICA, 1983

ISBN: 0-88139-001-1

ACKNOWLEDGEMENTS:

Typing, Transcribing, and Cover Design: Bhikshuni Heng Liang

Typing and Layout: Bhikshuni Heng Chia

Typing: Bhikshuni Heng Ming

Proofing: Bhikshuni Heng Chü, Bhikshuni Heng Bin, Bhikshuni Heng Chia, Linda Cole and Sari Epstein

Paste Up: Bhikshuni Heng Ch'ih, Bhikshuni Heng Chia, Amy Dickerson and Thanh Binh Thi Lam

Photograph of tree limb in "Sticky Love," by Alan Nicholson.

Translated by the BUDDHIST TEXT TRANSLATION SOCIETY

Primary Translation of Lectures of the Venerable Abbot Hua by:

  Bhikshu Heng Kuan
  Bhikshuni Heng Ch'ih
  Bhikshuni Heng Hsien
  Bhikshuni Heng Tao
  Bhikshu Heng Tso
  Ronald B. Epstein
  Terri Nicholson
  Bhikshu Heng Kung
  David Rounds
  Bhikshu Heng Wu
  Bhikshuni Heng Tsai
  Bhikshuni Heng Duan
  Bhikshuni Heng Lyan
  Bhikshuni Heng Chü
  Bhikshuni Heng Ming
  Bhikshuni Heng Liang
  Bhikshuni Heng Chia

FOR INFORMATION AND BOOKSALES CONTACT:

GOLD MOUNTAIN MONASTERY, 1731-15th Street,
   San Francisco, California 94103 (415) 861-9672
                                                 (415) 626-4204
GOLD WHEEL TEMPLE, 1728 West 6th Street,
   Los Angeles, California 90017 (213) 483-7497
                                                 (213) 258-6177
CITY OF TEN THOUSAND BUDDHAS, P.O. Box 217,
   Talmage, California 95481 (707) 462-0939
                                        (707) 462-9945

POSTAGE & HANDLING

United States: $1.25 for the first book and $.40 for each additional book. All publications are sent via special fourth class. Allow from 4 days to 2 weeks for delivery.

International: $1.50 for the first book and $.75 for each additional book. All publications are sent via 'book rate' or direct mail sack (surface). For countries, such as Indonesia and Malaysia, in which parcels may be lost, we suggest orders be sent via registered mail for an additional $3.25 per parcel of 10 books each. We cannot be responsible for parcels lost in the mail. Allow 6 to 8 weeks for delivery.

The rates noted above for postage and handling are given as an indication of actual costs. On large orders purchasers may wish to submit their order for a more precise estimate of postage and handling costs.

All orders require pre-payment before they will be processed.

All rights reserved including the right to reproduce this book or transmit it in any form or by any means electronic or mechanical, including photocopy, recording, or any information storage and retrieval system, except for the inclusion of brief quotations in a review.

TABLE OF CONTENTS

THE FIVE PRINCIPLES	1
KARMIC OBSTACLES	6
SINCERITY EVOKES A RESPONSE	9
FAITH	14
HOW THE FOX IMMORTAL TOOK REFUGE	16
THE MORE THE BETTER	23
ON WAY-VIRTUE	24
ON VIRTUE	27
THE SEVEN EMOTIONS AND TEN INJURIES	29
A WORLD INFESTED WITH POISONOUS SNAKES	32
WHEN THE CAUSE-GROUND IS NOT TRUE, THE RESULT WILL BE CROOKED	33
LIFE AT THE CITY OF TEN THOUSAND BUDDHAS	37
ALL FROM A SINGLE THOUGHT	41
DON'T SELL YOUR CULTIVATION	43
THE TEN DHARMA REALMS ARE NOT BEYOND A SINGLE THOUGHT	46
ZERO	49
DIFFUSE THE ATOM BOMB IN YOUR MIND...GET OUT OF THE TURNING WHEEL	55
FIRST, CURE THE CANCER OF YOUR OWN MIND	58
WHITE UNIVERSE	61
THE THREE CORPSE SPIRITS AND NINE WORMS	66
DO THE REAL THING AND DO IT WELL	71
TO CULTIVATE, GET RID OF YOUR EMOTIONS	73
THE PRECEPT SASH	76
THE WAY HAS TO BE PRACTICED	80
A SINGLE THOUGHT	86
TRUE REPENTANCE AND REFORM	87
UNIVERSAL WORTHY BODHISATTVA'S VERSE OF REPENTANCE AND REFORM	87
THE JOY OF NOT SEEKING	97

THE SECRETS OF HEAVEN AND EARTH	98
DHARMA-SELECTING EYE	102
FLAVORFUL CH'AN	104
THE TRUE WITHIN THE TRUE	107
STICKY LOVE	113
PRECEPTS, SAMADHI AND WISDOM	117
DON'T HAVE FOX DOUBTS	119
WHEN PEOPLE DON'T LIKE YOU	121
NEWS FROM CHINA: THE FIVE EYES	122
SCIENCE: BOON OR BANE?	123
...ON THE SHURANGAMA MANTRA	124
THESE SIMPLE VERSES: THE SHURANGAMA MANTRA	125
CONCENTRATION	127
TURN AFFLICTIONS INTO BODHI	129
KEEP THE PRECEPTS	131
ON THE GREAT COMPASSION MANTRA	133
THE TRICKY GEOMANCIST	134
AT THE CITY OF TEN THOUSAND BUDDHAS WE SHOULD CULTIVATE THE WAY	135
EARTH STORE BODHISATTVA	136
ON TOP OF WONDERFUL ENLIGHTENMENT MOUNTAIN, THE BUDDHA NODS HIS HEAD AND SMILES	140
IF YOU DON'T SEEK THE GREAT WAY, YOU AREN'T A GREAT HERO	141
PATIENCE	143
HELP OTHER WAY PLACES	145
DON'T CHEAT YOURSELF	145
THE ETERNAL BUDDHANATURE	149

Namo Shakyamuni Buddha

Buddhist Text Translation Society
Eight Regulations

A translator must free himself or herself from the motives of personal fame and reputation.

A translator must cultivate an attitude free from arrogance and conceit.

A translator must refrain from aggrandizing himself or herself and denigrating others.

A translator must not establish himself or herself as the standard of correctness and suppress the work of others with his or her faultfinding.

A translator must take the Buddha-mind as his or her own mind.

A translator must use the wisdom of the Selective Dharma Eye to determine true principles.

A translator must request the Elder Virtuous Ones of the ten directions to certify his or her translations.

A translator must endeavor to propagate the teachings by printing sutras, shastra texts, and vinaya texts when the translations are certified as being correct.

TRIPITAKA MASTER HUA

HEREIN LIES THE TREASURE-TROVE

THE FIVE PRINCIPLES

People who like to recite the Buddha's name are attending the Buddha Recitation Session. And those people who like to sit in meditation and investigate Ch'an, are attending the Ch'an Session. Then there are others who don't like to recite the Buddha's name nor do they like to sit in Ch'an, and so they are conducting their own Lazy Session, or they are holding a "Sleeping Session." Lazy Sessions and Sleeping Sessions are novel names, but actually, there's a lot of wisdom behind these names. In fact, people who like to be lazy are prevented from doing so by their own minds. Despite themselves, their brains keep on working--their minds generate a lot of false thinking. When you false think, you get caught on the turning gears of your mind that causes you to revolve in the six paths, turning around without cease. Originally, you wanted to be lazy, but in doing so, you end up taxing your brain even more. You waste no small amount of energy in having random thoughts and you end up even more tired and more lazy. You get lethargic and feel that everything is meaningless.

Those who are having Sleeping Sessions dream away, and in their dreams they might get rich, or they might become poor. In other dreams, they become big magistrates, while in other dreams they become beggars. In some dreams they see tigers, in others, dream about poisonous snakes; even within their dreams they aren't peaceful. So although you may want to have a Sleeping Session, you can't manage it-- it just doesn't work. Since you don't know how to apply your effort, no matter what you do, it doesn't turn out right. But for those who know how to apply their effort, no matter what they do, it turns out well.

Sitting Ch'an is a way to apply effort, and reciting the Buddha's name is also a way to apply effort. Even when people are being lazy, they are applying effort; and when they are asleep, they are also applying effort. Those are all ways in which one can apply one's effort. Even if you fall asleep, if you dream that you are bowing and reciting Sutras, that is a way in which you can still apply effort. And if you are being lazy by studying the Sutras or reading the Sutras instead of attending the intensive sessions, that's another way of applying effort.

So, at the City of Ten Thousand Buddhas, you can apply your effort by investigating Ch'an, or studying the Sutras, investigating the Vinaya, cultivating the Secret School, or practicing the Pure Land. It's all very natural. You don't have to feel embarrassed about it. Even if you are sleeping and being lazy, it's still a good thing, because if you are being lazy, then you won't go to the trouble of stealing things, and in that way you will be holding the Precepts. And while you are asleep you won't be able to kill people, so that's also keeping the Precepts. So, when we recite the Buddha's name, or investigate Ch'an, or study the Precepts, or study the Secret School, or study the Teachings, those are all ways to hold the Precepts. You hold the Precepts against killing, against stealing, against sexual misconduct, against uttering false speech, and against taking intoxicants. That's what's known as holding the Five Precepts.

Superficially, it may not appear that you are holding the Precepts, but you're actually holding without the appearance of holding them. Without calling it "holding Precepts," you are still holding the Precepts. So, at the City of Ten Thousand Buddhas, you can use whatever effort you want to. The only criterion is that when you use effort, you should be able to pick it up and put it down. That is, you should get involved in whatever Dharma door you study, and you should do well in whatever it is you are supposed to be doing. That's the correct way. Those who investigate Ch'an should investigate very attentively, and those who recite the Buddha's name should be diligent and mindful, and those who study and recite the Sutras should do so with vigor and respect. Those who study the Precepts should do so with a very sincere and straight mind. And those who practice the Secret School should be persevering in their practice.

Let's take a look at those who study the Secret School. We might investigate why people who study the Secret School can eventually become mice. Once they understand the principles behind this, they may open a small bit of enlightenment. When one opens enlightenment, it can be a small enlightenment or a great enlightenment. In this case, with just a small bit of enlightenment, they may come to understand some true principle.

At the City of Ten Thousand Buddhas we investigate the Five Principles which are just another name for the Five Precepts. First, there's no contention here, and so there's no killing. Why is it that people kill? It's because they contend. "You die and I live." The reason why people do so much killing is that their mind of contention has gone berserk. To have no contention is to not kill.

The second principle is to have no greed, which means no stealing. Why is it that people steal things? It's because of greed. If there's no greed what would anyone want to steal? Third, where there's no seeking, there's no desire. The mind of desire is the mind that seeks. Women look for boyfriends and men look for girlfriends. They are hot in pursuit of each other. And not only do they seek each other, but they chase after all kinds of material objects as well. Without any seeking, what desire would there be? Of what use would a handsome man be to you? And a beautiful woman is just a stinking skin-bag with flesh in it--what's so hot about that? If you don't seek for things, you won't break the Precepts against sexual misconduct.

The fourth principle is to have no selfishness and it relates to the fourth Precept, that of false speech. Why do people lie? Because their selfish minds go crazy. They are afraid of losing whatever benefits might come their way, and so they cheat people and lie. They think that if they lie they will be able to keep people from recognizing what they are up to and thereby won't lose their benefits.

Finally, selfishness leads to seeking self-benefit. Not seeking self-benefit coincides with the precept against taking intoxicants. Why do people take intoxicants? It is because their selfishness is so extreme, they lose their sense of right and wrong in their pursuit of self-indulgence. Once addicted to the fast but false high that intoxicants bring on, they get so spaced out they feel as if they were being born in the Land of Ultimate Bliss and becoming immortal. For example, when they get drunk, inevitably, their lust arises and having lost their sense of propriety, they do whatever they want. Intoxicants such as liquor and wine aid their practice of lust and so people drink and smoke even more in an attempt to derive sexual pleasure. This is motivated by the desire for self-benefit.

People who take intoxicants might argue that they are just doing it to aid their bodies, but deep down inside they know it is prompted by desire for self-benefit. They take wine with the excuse that they want to increase their circulation, but then they get drunk and forget everything. It's like getting high on opium. Therefore, not taking intoxicants is the same as not being self-benefitting.

So, these Five Principles are just another name for the Five Precepts. Why don't I just call them the Five Precepts? Because people are so used to hearing about the Five Precepts that when you talk about not killing, not stealing, not committing sexual misconduct, not using false speech, and not taking intoxicants, their response is "I already *know* that; what are you telling *me* for?" So now, the names have just been changed to:

        No Contention
        No Greed
        No Self-seeking
        No Selfishness
        No Self-benefitting

But even though people hear about these, and think they understand them, there are very few who can actually put them into practice. Now I want to reiterate what I've just said:

1. No killing is just non-contention.
2. No stealing is just no greed.
3. No sexual misconduct is just not self-seeking.
4. No false speech is just not being selfish.
5. No taking of intoxicants is just not seeking self-benefit.

    Now, if you think that what I have spoken is incorrect, or if you have a better idea, you can speak up. Those people who have been investigating Ch'an can talk about their awakenings and those who have been doing the recitation session can talk about the samadhis they have entered. Someone is thinking, "I had a state. What kind of state? When I sat in Ch'an, my legs began to *really* hurt! I couldn't stand it. And no matter what I said to them, they wouldn't listen to me. They told me not to sit in Ch'an." Don't be turned by that state. Pain is a very normal thing. The more pain, the better. You should know that you will not die from pain, but you should endure pain as if willing to die from it. If you have that kind of determination, the pain will be defeated and run away. Someone else says, " I had a state. My state isn't pain, however, when I sit, I fall asleep. I fall asleep and then I hit my head against the wall and get a big bump on my head. That's the kind of state I'm having." That kind of state is really good. That means that you have a really hard head! The wall is no match for your head, so when you hit your head against the wall, it made a big bump on it. But you shouldn't pay any attention to it. Just continue to work on developing some samadhi.
    Another person thinks, "I can't get my mind off food. I sit there and think,'is it time for lunch yet?' or, 'Oh, I am going to go into the kitchen and check it out and see if there's anything good to eat, because I don't know whether the cooks have cooked anything good or not.'"

QUESTION: During the sit if one hears the sound of recitation of the Buddha's name, what should one do? When I sit, in my mind I recite the Buddha's name and I can hear a lot of other people reciting the Buddha's name at the same time and I don't know whether to follow it or reject it. Can the Pure Land and Ch'an be combined together in that way?

ANSWER: When you are in a recitation session, it should be that the inside reciting and the outside reciting are the same, so that all external sounds merge and become the recitation of the Buddha's name. But if you are sitting in Ch'an, you shouldn't be listening to the sounds of the recitation of the Buddha's name. When you are sitting in Ch'an, you should be sitting in Ch'an. These are two separate Dharma doors. When you are sitting in Ch'an and you hear the sound of recitation of the Buddha's name, if you follow that sound and become attached, it's easy to get off the wrong road. It's easy to catch a demon. When you are supposed to be reciting the Buddha's name and you hear other voices reciting the name, it is not the case that you are going to catch a demon, because when you are truly reciting the Buddha's name,

The wind blows and the water flows;
Everything is reciting the Buddha's name.

The water is reciting the Buddha's name and the wind is reciting the Buddha's name, too. The bell sounds out the Buddha's name--everything from the four directions is reciting the Buddha's name. But if you are sitting in Ch'an and you hear the recitation of the Buddha's name, you shouldn't be turned by it. Pure Land and Ch'an are two different methods of practice.

QUESTION: When sitting in Ch'an, when I hear voices reciting the Buddha's name, I follow along with it and use it as a way to stop my false thinking.

ANSWER: If you are investigating Ch'an and hear the recitation of the Buddha's name, it's okay to use it in that way, but you shouldn't investigate it. When you investigate Ch'an, you should investigate "Who is mindful of the Buddha?" You look for the "Who," the one who is being mindful of the Buddha's name. But if you are reciting the Buddha's name and you hear other voices reciting, but you remain unattached to the state, then there's no obstruction involved.

KARMIC OBSTACLES

The world has a coming into being, a dwelling, decaying, and becoming empty. Human life has birth, old age, sickness, and death. One increase and one decrease of our world is called a kalpa. Every hundred years during the period of increase, the average human lifespan increases one year, and the average height increases one inch. Beginning with a lifespan of ten years, it continues to increase to 84,000 years, then it begins to decrease. Every hundred years during a period of decrease, the average lifespan decreases one year and the average height decreases one inch. One thousand of these kalpas is called a small kalpa. Twenty small kalpas make a middle-sized kalpa, and four middle-sized kalpas make a large kalpa. A world comes into being for 20 small kalpas and dwells for 20 small kalpas, declines for 20 small kalpas, and goes empty for 20 small kalpas. So coming into being, dwelling, decaying, and emptiness--each a middle-sized kalpa in length--together make a large kalpa. The time of a large kalpa is long. It's not something that can be conceptualized with ordinary human intelligence.

The human lifespan is only several decades long. From birth through the time of adulthood is only 20 years. This corresponds to the 20 small kalpas it takes for a world to come into being. Aging, sickness, and death correspond to dwelling, decaying, and emptiness. So the period of aging is another 20 years, from the ages of 20 to 40. These are the years of living in the world when we can accomplish something. This corresponds to the 20 kalpas' period of dwelling. After dwelling comes change or decay. This corresponds to the time of sickness, from ages 40 to 60. During this time, the eyes go bad, the ears become dull, and the teeth begin to fall out. The back and legs become painful. Every kind of small illness hits. The time of decay takes 20 small kalpas. Then comes emptiness, which corresponds to death. Death usually occurs for people during the period of 60 to 80 years. At this time, no matter how much money you may have, you can't take it with you. In the cycle of worlds, emptiness continues for 20 small kalpas as well. So one's life is just like coming into being, dwelling, decaying, and emptiness.

With the situation as it is, those who can genuinely understand are few. Those who genuinely cultivate are also few. Most people just muddle through, letting the time go by in vain. From the day of birth to the day of death, one has no idea what one is doing here. So one's lifetime passes by. Most of humanity is just about like this. If within such a situation one can find a path of light and know "Where I have come from and where I am going to when I leave," it counts as not being a muddled human being. But if one fails to see the light, then, "when coming one is muddled, when going one is confused, and in-between, one passes through a human life in vain."

That isn't as good as "not coming and not going." It's best to just not come and not go, then there's no confusion, sadness, or trouble. But most people are dragged about by their karma. They come into this world to repay their debts and undergo the retribution due them. All the various kinds of karma they have created in the past and the retribution that they receive in this life, as it's said, form a "net of karma woven together." So, in this world, all kinds of causes and conditions get woven into a net of karma--all sorts of situations come together to form our very confused and muddled lives. But people don't realize this and go right on thinking that this place is very interesting. They don't know enough to look for a way to put an end to birth and death and be liberated from the turning wheel. This is a very pitiful situation.

Speaking on this subject brings to mind a person who was, during his lifetime, the richest man in the world. He had more money than anyone else. He possessed the most jewels, gold, and silver in the world. Because he was fond of jewels, when his eldest son was born, he named him "Diamond." And because he liked gold, when his second son was born, he named him "Gold." After several more years he had another son, and since he had no real aversion to silver, he named his third son "Silver." After several more years he had another son, and without knowing why, he gave that son the name "Karmic Obstructions." He sired four sons, and they all grew up and got their own households and professions.

Then the richest man in the world became ill. He had a stroke and became paralyzed on one side of his body. So, he asked his eldest son, Diamond, to care for him.

Diamond said, "No. Go ask your second eldest son." So he asked his second eldest son to care for him.

Gold said, "No. Ask Silver." So he asked his third son, Silver, to take care of him.

Silver replied, "I'm afraid it's not okay. I still have a lot of my own affairs to take care of because I haven't really been completely successful in my career, so I can't take care of you."

So, he asked Karmic Obstacles. Karmic Obstacles was really obedient, and took care of him. Because of the kind of paralysis he had, it was difficult for the richest man in the world to eat, and others had to feed him and help him to the toilet. After a period of time, not even Karmic Obstacles paid any attention to him, and his illness got so severe that he couldn't even eat or drink anything. So the richest man in the world knew that the time had probably come for him to die.

He called his eldest son to his side and said, "Diamond, Diamond, in this life I have raised you to manhood. Now my time to die has come. After death, I'll be very lonely. No one will come to visit me. How about coming along to die with me?"

When Diamond heard this, he said, "You're really an old muddled fellow. If you're going to die, then die a little sooner and get it over with! How can you expect to drag me along with you to accompany you in death? What a lot of nonsense!"

Diamond left and didn't pay any more attention to his father. The richest man in the world was really brokenhearted because Diamond wouldn't accompany him. He called Gold and said, "Gold, I've taken really good care of you. I raised you and now you are grown up. Now my time to die has come. How about accompanying me in death? Want to come along with me?"

Gold opened his eyes wide, stared at him and said, "If you must die, die a little sooner! I could not go with you, you're old and I am still young. How could I go with you?"

So the richest man called Silver and asked him if he would go off to die with him to keep him company.

Silver replied, "You old thing! I should beat you to death first! As old as you are and you still are up to mischief! How could I accompany you in death?" He too, wouldn't go with him.

The richest man in the world was utterly devastated and wept bitterly. Finally he called Karmic Obstacles, his fourth son, and said, "Karmic Obstacles, Karmic Obstacles, I really have a lot of causal conditions with you. Although you are the youngest, and although I love you the least, since I am about to die, will you come off to death with me?"

Karmic Obstacles said, "Fine, fine. I'll go along with you to die. No matter where you go, I'll follow."

So it's said:

> *Sallow, sallow, like a chicken's skin.*
> *Your hair is white, white like the crane.*
> *Look. Look. Just look at you.*
> *You're on your way out and can't even walk.*

SINCERITY EVOKES A RESPONSE

All of you have come from ten thousand miles away to the City of Ten Thousand Buddhas. This is Kuan Yin Bodhisattva's Way-place. Kuan Yin Bodhisattva immigrated from Putala (*P'u T'ou*), Mountain to open this Way-place and start Buddhism in the west. Not only did Kuan Yin Bodhisattva immigrate to America, but all the Patriarchs from East and West and from the Four Holy Mountains of China also immigrated to America. This is just an analogy because the Bodhisattva doesn't immigrate; he dwells everywhere. The Dharma body doesn't dwell anywhere, and yet pervades all places. Not only has Kuan Yin Bodhisattva come to the City of Ten Thousand Buddhas, but also Manjushri Bodhisattva, Earth Store Bodhisattva, and Universal Worthy Bodhisattva have come here too. All of you know that Kuan Yin Bodhisattva, Manjushri Bodhisattva, Earth Store Bodhisattva, and Universal Worthy Bodhisattva are the four great Bodhisattvas of the Four Holy Mountains in China. And now these four have come to America along with all the Buddhas and the Eight-fold Division of dragons and spirits.

All of you have come from ten thousand miles away to this Sagely City. It is by the compassionate vows of Kuan Yin Bodhisattva that you have come here. So after arriving here you should be very reverent, as though you were face to face with the Buddhas and Bodhisattvas, and you shouldn't be lax. Kuan Yin Bodhisattva has opened up the frontier and established Buddhism in the West. It's a very difficult task. Even though we say that Kuan Yin Bodhisattva has many response bodies, nonetheless, he has to work hard here. Kuan Yin started from 1976, 1977, 1978, 1979, 1980, 1981, 1982--six years already. Three years ago we opened the light on Kuan Yin's Way-place and more and more people arrived to bow to, and worship Kuan Yin Bodhisattva. Before we opened the light at the City of Ten Thousand Buddhas, he was busy day and night, until the year of 1979, when we opened the light. And now, in the fall of 1982, we have completed the Mountain Gate, and the Hall of Ten Thousand Buddhas; the Long-Life Hall and the Rebirth Hall are almost done. And a new Five-Contemplations Vegetarian Dining Hall that can seat 2000 has also been completed. Now it's time to start building the Jeweled Hall of Great Heroes. The width of this hall from east to west, including the sidewalks, will measure to 300 feet. If you don't include the sidewalks, it will measure 270 feet. From north to south it will measure 200 feet. To our knowledge, this is probably the largest Great Jeweled Hall of Heroes anywhere. Why do we want to build such a big Jeweled

Hall of Great Heroes? It's because America is a huge country and everything here should be big and up to universal standards. If we begin building the hall now, we can finish in three years. Also in the works is the Avatamsaka Wayplace--maybe that will take five or six years to finish, because it will be massive. When all of you go back to your homes, you should continue to bring forth sincere minds and after three years, you can come back again and attend the opening ceremonies for the Jeweled Hall of Great Heroes. Perhaps we can finish the Jeweled Pagoda, too.

It can also be said that all the great Buddhas and Bodhisattvas emit light which shines on this great Way-place of the City of Ten Thousand Buddhas. Are you aware that the air at the City of Ten Thousand Buddhas is different from the air outside the City? It's extremely pure and fresh and rejuvenating. So when you come here to the City, don't bring your habitual energy and bad habits along. Every day you should act as if you were face to face with the Buddhas and Bodhisattvas. You can't laugh and joke around and gossip. If you act that way, there's no value in coming here. And then it will be as the saying goes,

Under the auspicious mountain, there's no Way-place.

So don't do any muddled talking, laughing, and giggling, as if you were going to the movies or theater.

No matter who you are, you should follow the rules of the City. If you can maintain the rules and the precepts, then you can gain purity. The light of the Buddhas and Bodhisattvas will shine upon you and all your wishes will be fulfilled, and any disasters coming to you will be averted. Otherwise, if you don't have a mind of sincerity, there are places all over the world that have places for giggling and carrying on that you can go to. You don't have to come all the way here. If you don't bring forth utmost sincerity, then it's just a waste of your time and money.

You should bring forth a mind of repentance, bow to the Buddhas, and take cultivation as your main job. If you come to bow to the Buddhas and still can't cast away your habitual energies and faults, how dumb you are! You should also cast out the mind of greed and contention. Whatever you do, don't contend with anyone. Also, don't be greedy. When you are greedy, you are being unfair. When you have a mind of contention, you use it to exert force, and to oppress the weak.

Those who study the Buddhadharma don't contend with anyone, but cultivate patience instead. What do the Buddhas like to see in their disciples? They like to see disciples who have a mind of great sacrifice, who are truly able to renounce themselves and benefit others. Who can really do the great work of the Buddhas while remaining in the sea of suffering? Who can propagate the Buddhadharma within the Saha World? If you want to propagate the Buddhadharma, then you absolutely have to be proper in everything you do. As it is said,

> *When a person is proper, he doesn't have to give people orders and they will follow him of their own accord.*
> *But, if a person is not proper, then even if he forces people, they will not comply.*

Be a good example, not a bad one. Make yourselves good models for everyone to follow. If you are proper, then you don't need to order people around. They will still practice after you and follow you. You won't need to use all kinds of tricky methods to oppress people so that they follow you. If you are not proper yourself but still greedy and contentious, selfish, and self-benefitting, then you cannot teach others not to be greedy, not to be contentious, not to be selfish, and not to be self-benefitting. In that case, it won't work. So, if a person is not proper, even if he orders others around, they won't obey. Then no matter what he tries to teach people to do, they won't listen to him.

I will tell you something. While at the City of Ten Thousand Buddhas, I don't mind anyone else's business or try to control anyone else. Whatever people like to do, they can go ahead and do it. People bring forth the mind to protect the Way-place spontaneously, and do their jobs and perform services for the Way-place. I don't control a single one of them. So you see, all the cultivators at the City of Ten Thousand Buddhas cultivate vigorously from day to night, and most of them eat only one meal a day. They also have to do a lot of Buddha affairs. For the sake of the Buddhadharma, they forget their bodies, and offer up their souls.

So, before opening the light, we had people who used saws to trim the trees, and some of them hurt their fingers, but very fortunately, they didn't cut any of their fingers off. This is a response from Kuan Yin Bodhisattva. Also, someone sprained his leg, but again, very fortunately, it didn't get broken. That is just another response from Kuan Yin Bodhisattva. There weren't any serious accidents. His leg didn't get broken. Another worker on the outside was doing the same job. He too hurt his legs and even after two months rest, he may not recover. At this big Way-place we have so many projects going on, but none of us get hurt. This just shows that Kuan Yin Bodhisattva protects us at all times.

Also, on the 22nd and 23rd, two people from San Francisco were coming to the City of Ten Thousand Buddhas. About twenty miles from here, their car got into an accident. It crashed. But the two people in the car didn't get scratched. That's another example of the response of Kuan Yin Bodhisattva. These kinds of responses happen every day at the City. They are all inconceivable. They are limitless and it cannot be spoken to exhaustion. It's too much.

You have all arrived at the mountain of jewels. You shouldn't go back home empty-handed. You should bring forth a sincere mind to worship the Buddhas. No matter where you are, whether in the Dorm or in the Guest Hall, in your daily affairs, all the Buddhas and Bodhisattvas and Sages are watching you. They say, "Take a look at him. What's he doing? Has he come here with a sincere mind? What are the reasons for his coming here? Does he bring forth a mind of greed? Does he come here and bow to the Buddhas in hopes of getting rich? Does he expect to win the sweepstakes when he leaves? Does he have thoughts like that or not?"

All the Sages, the Buddhas, and Bodhisattvas are testing you. You don't want to think whatever you do, say, or think is not known to them. The Buddhas and Bodhisattvas know about whatever you think in your mind. So if you have come here because of your sickness, you have to bring forth a sincere mind and bow to the Buddhas. Then, naturally, your sickness will be eradicated. In the past, lots of people have come here to bow to Kuan Yin Bodhisattva, and although they had very serious cases of cancer, they got well. I don't remember off-hand how many people came here with that kind of sickness, but they all got well. So if you have a sincere mind, there will be a response. Otherwise, there won't be any response. You can't blame the Bodhisattvas for not protecting you. It's because you don't have a true mind. You can't say, "I have come from so far away and spent so much money, how can you say I don't have a sincere mind?" Yes. You used a lot of money to get here, and that indicates a certain amount of sincerity. But once you get here, if you are sloppy, then it will be of no use at all.

So all of you, bring forth your most sincere, reverent and respectful minds and bow to the City of Ten Thousand Buddhas. I will tell you that I don't know how to cure people's sicknesses. I just borrow the power of Kuan Yin Bodhisattva. Kuan Yin Bodhisattva gives me the authority and says whatever sickness you have, when you come here, you will get well. The only stipulation is that you bring forth a sincere and true mind.

In Hong Kong, at the Western Bliss Gardens, there was a mother who brought her five year old child who couldn't walk. Everywhere he went, his mother had to carry him. Then his mother heard someone say that I knew how to cure illnesses. So she came to see me and I told her, "I don't know how to cure people's sicknesses. Instead, you should bow sincerely to the Buddhas. If you are sincere in your bowing to the Buddhas, then your child's sickness will get better." On Ma An Shan, there are 300 steps leading up to the temple, and she bowed everyday from the bottom to the top, one bow for every step; not just once every three steps. She bowed almost a half year and the child got well--he recovered. He didn't know the reason why he recovered. I didn't pass out any kind of medicine. That woman just bowed with her child from the bottom of the mountain to the top of the mountain and then the child got well. What's the reason behind this? It was because of her sincerity and so she had this kind of response. So if you come and bow to Kuan Yin Bodhisattva, those who have anger become happy; and the dead ones come back to life. If you say this is false and not true, you should know that all the Buddhas don't tell lies. All of you should deeply understand this. If you don't get a response, it just shows that you don't have enough sincerity. This is because when you are outside, you are cheating people all of the time, and then when you come here, you try to use the same mind to try to cheat the Buddhas and Bodhisattvas. But you can't cheat the Buddhas and Bodhisattvas at all. Someone's thinking, "I don't like what the Abbot is saying. It upsets me a lot." Then don't listen!

FAITH

--Bhikshu Heng Kuan

The greatest good and the greatest evil both come forth from a single thought. But many don't know and many don't believe. In the West we are taught to dispassionately investigate things and prove their validity through analytical probing. To be objective--that's the method of education that is taught in our school systems. This is just using a doubting mind to investigate things. You look at things from all sides and then decide whether they are true or false. As a result, people are taught to look at society, and religion in this same way. So even though a lot of people still have good roots, they don't have any true or worthwhile educational values, and so they consistently do a lot of things without knowing why they are doing them. They trust in their doubting minds which are not based on truth and principle. They use something false--the false, doubting mind--to get at what's true. How can you get the true by using the false? From this relative point of view, you can't get the true with the false. True is true and false is false.

At Dharma Realm Buddhist University, we teach people that it's possible to put this doubting mind aside and study true principle and put it into practice. But in order to do that, a totally sincere mind is the major criterion. If we can just put to rest our doubting minds, suspend our beliefs and set them aside, pick up the principles of the Sutras and put them into practice, then we can get some pretty remarkable results. But one can't cheat oneself and use a doubting mind to practice, because that won't work. If one finds it difficult to put one's doubts aside, then one should use a *totally* doubting mind: doubt the mountains, the rivers and the great earth; doubt what's even on the inside; doubt all of it. That's what's done in the practice of Ch'an. That's the only way to use the doubting mind, until one doubts doubt itself--using poison to counteract poison. But the Western scientific mind finds it difficult to believe. So although many people hear the principles of the Sutras and think they are pretty good, nonetheless, there aren't many who can suspend their doubts long enough to try the practices out. And if one can try them out with a sincere mind, and achieve some results--because that's what will happen--then one can obtain pure faith and find it easier to cultivate. Faith is the source of the Way, mother of all merit and virtue. It's not the case that there are some who can believe and others who just can't. However, it is necessary to suspend one's doubts and try the methods out. Earth Store Bodhisattva is basically just a person. But he decided long ago that he would stop being selfish and help others. So we shouldn't think of Earth Store Bodhisattva as being too far away and too out-of-sight. It's just that most people only think of themselves and their own families and property. But if one can *think* like Earth Store Bodhisattva, they can *become* like Earth Store Bodhisattva. If one can bring forth such faith in just the space of a single meal, one can get out of the evil paths. Even though karma is not off by a hair, nonetheless, Earth Store Bodhisattva has made vast vows to save all living beings, and although we've made our own karma and must undergo the retribution, there is no principle in the Sutras that says that Earth Store Bodhisattva can't rescue us. And so, though the fruits of our karma may be severe, the karma of Earth Store Bodhisattva can overcome ours.

HOW THE FOX IMMORTAL TOOK REFUGE

Those who study the Buddhadharma should cause the Buddhadharma to flourish and expand day by day; they shouldn't cause the Buddhadharma to decline day by day. How can we cause Buddhism to flourish and increase day by day? First, we have to improve our character; we have to make a good foundation. If you make a good foundation, then no matter what kind of big building or skyscraper you build on it, it will never collapse. But if the foundation is not good, then there's no way to build a big building or skyscraper on it. If we want to cause Buddhism to increase and flourish, it's like building a multi-storied pavilion that has floor after floor without end--a jeweled tower. But first we must complete the foundation, that is, make our character upright and establish our virtue. We should not be stingy or narrow-minded. Instead we should be very broad minded so that our nature encompasses empty space and our measure becomes as great as world-realms to the number of Ganges River sands. Everyone think about this. Empty space does not only contain good energy. There are world realms as many as the sands in the Ganges River--all kinds of different worlds--and within these worlds dwell an endless variety of creatures of all different shapes and colors. There are good ones and bad ones. And we need to include them within the measure of our mind.

When we are making our character solid and establishing our virtue, we need to really work hard, pay no attention to ourselves, but take care of others instead. We need to admit our faults and go toward the good. Don't have any attachment toward yourself, don't have a mark of self. Don't look at yourself as being so important. This is all part of establishing a firm foundation for the Way. If you make your foundation strong in this way, then even if you don't seek for the Buddhadharma to increase and flourish, it will still increase and flourish. Even if you don't go around thinking about propagating the Buddhadharma, nonetheless, the Buddhadharma will naturally increase and flourish and expand.

I remember, when I was seventeen or eighteen years old, in Dong Bei, a Province in Manchuria where I lived, there was the Bei Yin River. Bei means "the back," and yin is the yin of yin/yang. During the time of the Japanese occupation, the Japanese constructed a great incinerator for destroying humanity. Putting people in this huge cauldron was even worse than putting them in a rotisserie, like the ones they use for roasting chickens. At least a rotisserie leaves the bones intact, and you can still see the semblance of the chicken's body. But when people were boiled in this huge cauldron, their bodies were burnt to a crisp so that even their flesh and bones disappeared. Where were these people taken from? They were all Dong Bei people. Anyone who was at all questionable in the eyes of the Japanese or whom they thought were the slightest bit unbeneficial to them, they would round up such a person so that he would suddenly vanish into thin air. Questionable people were herded into railroad cars. The train would stop right by the entrance to the huge incinerator. The Japanese soldiers would open up the railroad car door and herd flocks of people right into the cauldron where they were fried alive. Isn't that just like hell on earth? Like the Hell of Boiling Soup? It was never known how many people were killed in this way. There's no way to ever know--probably tens of thousands.

Originally that compound was a winery, but the Japanese took it over and occupied it because the buildings were quite well made and they set this place up to accommodate the destruction of all questionable Chung Kuo citizens. Now at that time there was a fox immortal--a good hearted and sagely fox immortal--who couldn't bear the bane that the people of China were going through. He wanted revenge for the Chung Kuo people. So he very often appeared in a transformation body of an old man with white hair and a long white beard. He appeared both in the daytime and at night. Whenever he appeared, the Japanese soldiers shot at him with their rifles, because no unauthorized person was allowed to go inside the compound. If anyone without permission for being there was seen, they were considered to be spies and shot to death right on the spot. But when they took shots at this white haired old man, he wasn't afraid. When they shot at him he just turned around and headed straight for the ammunition storehouse and blew it up. After the first time this happened the Japanese still weren't very careful, so it happened again, but they still weren't careful. It continued to happen, it's not known how many times, so that many Japanese soldiers were killed, blown up. Finally they became afraid to live in the compound anymore. Since they no longer wanted the place for themselves, for fear that others would move in and use it, they destroyed the buildings before they left, and then they retreated from that place.

Since everyone in the surrounding area knew that they had left because of the appearance of the fox immortal, some of those folks went to that area to seek medicine from the fox immortal so as to cure their illnesses. This fox immortal was very compassionate and gave them medicine. Those people would take a tea cup or a rice bowl, cover it with a piece of red cloth and go to that spot to seek medicine. They would kneel there and pray for the medicine for five or ten or twenty minutes and then they'd lift the red cloth and find the medicine in their bowl. Sometimes they'd find powdered medicine, or various other forms of efficacious medicine. Word of this miracle-cure spread from one person to ten people, from ten people to a thousand and so on until all the people for a thousand miles around came to seek for medicine at that place. It became a hub of activity.

At that time, because my mother was sick, I went to seek for medicine, too. And to demonstrate my sincerity, I knelt there so that the immortal would give me medicine for my mother. I knelt for a day and nothing happened. I knelt for two days and still nothing happened. Even after three days of kneeling like that, there was still no response. Not getting any response after three days--I had knelt for three days, mind you, so it couldn't be said that I lacked sincerity--I couldn't understand why there was no response. I blamed myself for not being sincere enough. I certainly didn't think, "Fox immortal, you aren't being compassionate with me," and go off unhappy. I wasn't unhappy with him. I just blamed myself for not being filial enough. Then I went and bought some medicinal herbs. Since I understood the nature of medicinal herbs, when my mother took the herbs, she got well.

Afterward, bit by bit, I studied and inquired into the Buddhadharma, but for my brothers and sisters and the rest of my six close relatives, I did not explain the Buddhadharma. Since I didn't discuss the Buddhadharma with them, what did we talk about? I didn't say anything to them. Instead, I let my actions speak. For instance, the things that most people liked, I didn't like. The things that most people sought after, I didn't seek after. Most people tried to get off cheap, but I wasn't greedy for that. As I let my actions speak in these various ways for them, the people in my immediate family didn't know what to make of it. They felt, "This person is really strange"; they didn't dare ask me about what I was doing, and I didn't say anything to them. My brothers and sisters didn't understand me. Although they didn't understand me, I didn't think, "How can I find some way to take them across?" I didn't think about that because I was going out from my home and traveling all over giving lectures for people on the Buddhadharma. When people asked me to speak, I spoke. At the age of sixteen, I was already lecturing on the *Vajra Sutra* and the *Sixth Patriarch Sutra*. Although I didn't know many characters, I dared to explain the Sutras to people, but my immediate relatives didn't know anything about this. After my mother passed away, I went forth from the home life and still my brothers and sisters didn't know what I was all about; they thought I was very strange. Later, I had a relative--the husband of my second eldest sister--who did this and that and for some unknown reason became possessed by this fox immortal. The fox immortal used his body to speak. He said to my second eldest sister, "Do you know that your younger brother went to such and such a temple to leave the home life? I and my retinue want to take refuge with him. Please go and tell him that we want to take refuge with him and bow to him as our teacher."

When my second eldest sister heard that she was very surprised. When she gave me this news I related to her the incident of my seeking for the medicine. And then I asked her husband, "Which fox immortal are you?"

He said that he was the fox immortal who had caused the Japanese to be driven out, and then he told me he wanted to take refuge with the Triple Jewel.

I said, "Well, if you think that's what you want to do it's all right with me." Then I asked, "Since you are that very fox immortal, then tell me, why didn't you give me medicine when I went seeking it from you?"

He said, "Oh, I'm truly sorry, but I wasn't able to come before you. While you were kneeling there, so many Dharma protectors and wholesome spirits were all around you, front and back, protecting you, that I couldn't get near you even if I had wanted to give you the medicine. There was no way to do it."

So I said, "Oh, since that was the case, I'll give you refuge." And so I administered the three refuges for him. Not only that, but since my brothers and sisters saw that the fox immortal took refuge with me, they all came and took refuge with me too--all my brothers and sisters, in-laws and so on--they all came and took refuge. I hadn't spoken any Buddhadharma for them and it had never occured to me that my encounter with the fox immortal could cause them to take refuge with the Buddhadharma. I also had not exhorted my father to believe in the Buddhadharma, but eventually my father came to live at the monastery and bowed to the Buddha. So, if you want to take people across, the most important thing to do is to establish your own virtue and character and make a good foundation. Then, quite imperceptibly, a power of response will manifest, which will influence people.

This is for sure. This is a series of events from the time before I went forth from the home life.

I'll tell you about what happened after I left home. I went to the temple and everyone looked down on me. My elder Dharma brothers scolded me, and even my younger Dharma brothers scolded me--even the little kids in the monastery scolded me. Everyone bullied me all day long. It wasn't just an occasional thing. Not to mention scolding, they even beat me. I asked why they scolded me: no reason. I asked why they hit me: still no reason. The only answer I got was, "We want to scold you; we want to beat you." So at that time I took a lot of abuse from people, and even though I basically had a big temper, I was patient with it all. People scolded me and I didn't get angry; people hit me and I didn't lose my temper.

Not only did I not get angry or lose my temper, but within my heart I really thanked them for being my good knowing friends. Because of those experiences I had when I was young, I now advocate that when all of you are scolded you should not even realize it, and when you get struck, you shouldn't get afflicted. You should have no mark of a self, no mark of others, no mark of living beings, and no mark of a life span, to the point that the mind of the past will be unobtainable, the mind of the present will be unobtainable, and the mind of the future will be unobtainable. You will be able to see that the three minds--the mind of the present, the mind of the past, and the mind of the future--are all unobtainable and that the three marks are all empty. Then who will there be to get angry? Who will there be to get afflicted? If you can be that way, then you can cultivate. If you can't be that way, then you still have to practice...practice!

* * * * *

I will now tell you something and it's not an arrogant statement. Throughout the entire world, the City of Ten Thousand Buddhas is the place with the most proper and righteous energy. Why is this? It's because we want to turn the world from the bad to the good. The kind of things we do here are beyond the expectations of people. They can't even begin to conceive of what we are doing here. What do I mean? Because we want to benefit the entire world, with that aim in mind we can vastly expand our vision. In the near future, Buddhism will extend to the United States, and since this is an international country, there has to be a place that's big enough to accommodate many people. The

City of Ten Thousand Buddhas is big enough. It can accommodate ten thousand people. If you look throughout all of Asia, you won't find a Bodhimanda to the size of this scale. Some people say they want to do big things--the bigger the better. But when those very people come to the City of Ten Thousand Buddhas they get scared. They begin to act like a frog at the bottom of the well, looking up at the sky.

For instance, take our new dining hall. It should be big enough to use for the next ten years or so, but after that I don't know. We came here with an attitude of sacrifice. I came to the United States from Asia with nothing in my pockets, only with the wish to spread Buddhism throughout the entire world. I have had such an attitude all along, and it still remains the same.

Look at the schools of the City of Ten Thousand Buddhas. Their establishment was certainly not motivated by a wish to take money from people. Even the children's meals are free. Is it the case that we're "tossing out bricks to attract jade?" Offering something small hoping to attract something big? No. However, my expectations are really big. I want my students to be truly good people so that they will not contribute to the destruction of the world but will instead be of benefit to the world in the future.

"You always say that you don't want money, but yet you're coming up with such huge projects. How do you do it?" The only thing I have to do it with is my true heart. In the future we will use left home people in positions of administration, but if you want to put forth true effort, don't be seeking after fame and gain. There's no profiteering going on here. You should put forth your best effort to help the world. Some people claim that they want to help the world, but in the process, they manage to "skim the cream off the top"--they take a little for themselves; they take advantage of their positions.

Some of you here have known me for many years, and in all that time, have I ever cheated you in any way? Have I ever pulled tricks on you? If I have, then you should tell me and I will quickly change. If I haven't, then you should understand what I'm doing here, and bring forth your true heart to help.

Very soon there will be a lot of activities going on here--the opening of the Mountain Gate, purifying the boundaries for the Jeweled Hall of Great Heroes, a ribbon-cutting ceremony and opening the light on the Hall of Ten Thousand Buddhas and the opening of our new dining hall. There will be much activity. Whoever lives here should not lie back and take the whole thing as a big joke. Don't try to climb on conditions either, and kiss up to rich guests or try to set up good P.R. with influential people. That's cheap and vile conduct. The people of the City of Ten Thousand Buddhas always maintain a very lofty and pure air about them. They take public affairs as their own personal business and don't seek self-benefit. They use their true minds and do true things.

THE MORE THE BETTER

The Kuan Yin Session has been completed last week and the first week of the Ch'an session will soon be over. Starting from tomorrow, the people who are participating in the Ch'an Session will move to the Precept Platform and single-mindedly inquire into Ch'an, and here in the hall of the Ten Thousand Buddhas, we will begin another Buddha Recitation Session. This Ch'an Session is an experiment. It's the first of its kind. If you feel that you can take it, you can participate in the Ch'an Session, but if you feel you can't take it, you can participate in the Buddha Recitation Session. In either way you can put forth effort.

So, here at the City of Ten Thousand Buddhas at one place we can have Ch'an meditation and at another place, we can have a Buddha Recitation Session, and there are still other places where we can bow repentance ceremonies. At any one time we can have any number of different kinds of cultivation going on simultaneously. There's something called "the Water and Land Way-places." At such Way-places both the living and the dead attain benefit, as well as living beings on the land and in the water. For instance, the Venerable Master Hsü Yün held "Water and Land" Dharma assemblies in the 7th lunar month in Hsi Yün Monastery, Kuang T'ung Province. There was such a great response that the peach blossoms bloomed (this was late summer, early fall, and peach blossoms usually bloom in spring). Now, at the City of Ten Thousand Buddhas, it's just like having a "Water and Land Way-place."

At this Monastery, in many different places, there are people doing their work, and no one knows what anyone else is doing because it's such a big place. Since we have such a big place here, we can do whatever we like, everyone at the same time. We can have all kinds of Buddhist activities going on. Here at the City of Ten Thousand Buddhas we have Ch'an and the Teachings and the Vinaya School and the Esoteric School and the Pure Land School--we practice all those Dharma doors here. And the only fear is that you won't work hard in your cultivation. Our only fear is that you are all muddled and confused.

ON WAY-VIRTUE

Lao Tze said:

*When the superior person hears of the Way,
he diligently cultivates it.
When the mediocre person hears of the Way,
he grasps some and loses some.
When the inferior person hears of the Way,
he laughs aloud at it.
If it is not something he laughs aloud at,
it is not truly the Way.*

Of the Way, it is said:

*Open it out and it fills the six
 directions;
Roll it up and it hides away in the most
 secret place.*

It is big with nothing beyond it; small with nothing inside it. There is no person--indeed, no living being--who is not included in the Way. The Way is the nature--the basic substance of each one of us.

The Buddha said:

*All living beings have the Buddha-nature;
All can become Buddhas.*

It also can be said:

*All living beings have the Way;
All can accomplish their Way-karma.*

They can accomplish it, whether they be womb-born, egg-born, moisture-born or transformation-born; whether they fly, crawl, or swim--whichever of the four kinds of birth and nine realms of existence they belong to.

"Superior person" means an outstanding individual, a person with wisdom and deep, thick good roots. When such a person hears of the Way, "he diligently cultivates it."

Confucius said,

*If I hear of the Way in the morning,
 I can die in the evening with no regrets.*

"Hear of the Way" means to understand, to be enlightened to. All are replete with it; no one is without it. But we have

wandered away from the Way. The Way is the rules. If you
walk according to the rules, you are a person of the Way.
Precepts are the rules. The Way basically is a path to end
birth and death. It's the way to walk. But first you have
to close the door on birth and death. What's that door?
It's thoughts of desire--sexual desire. If you have those
thoughts, you've opened the door to birth and death. If you
cut off sexual desire, you can close the door on birth and
death.

When a superior person hears of the Way,
he diligently cultivates it.

He says, "Oh! It's like that! I should do it like that!
He returns to the source and seeks within himself. He returns the light around and shines within. He personally applies effort, like a hen sitting on her eggs, like a dragon
guarding its pearl, or like a cat stalking a mouse. He always maintains his practice, just as those animals maintain
their attentiveness. He cultivates and has no false thinking.

When a mediocre person hears of the Way,
he grasps some and loses some.

A "mediocre person" is someone who is half wise and half
stupid--an ordinary person. He seems to be what, in fact,
he is not. He becomes attached either to emptiness or to
existence. He doesn't know how to hold to the Middle Way.

When the inferior person hears of the Way,
he laughs aloud at it.

The "inferior person" is the stupidest of people. You tell
such a person to cut off sexual desire, to cultivate the
Way, to follow the rules, and to maintain the precepts. He
says, "That's a loser, that's too dumb," and laughs a big
belly laugh. "That's too stupid. How can you do without
that? Wealth, sex, fame, food, and sleep are great!" And
he laughs at "stupid" cultivators.

If it is not something he laughs aloud
at, it's not truly the Way.

Everyday I lecture Sutras and speak the Dharma. The most
important thing is to cut off sexual desire. The *Shurangama
Sutra* says it straight out:

If you don't get rid of lust,
You can't get out of the dust.

If you try to do it any other way,

> *It's like cooking sand to get rice.
> It can't be done.*

Cultivators should not be like ordinary, worldly people. We shouldn't be interested in what worldly people like or what they are greedy for. We should be different from worldly people in thought, word and deed. We should all know this.

In the beginning I allowed people to get along without following the rules. Now I've discovered that it won't work. Everyone must hold to the rules, follow the precepts, and cultivate the Way. If you leave home and don't hold to the rules, follow the precepts, and cultivate the Way, what use is there in leaving home? Take birthdays, for instance. Lay people celebrate them, but only once a year. However, there are left-home people who make a big deal of birthdays, allowing several celebrations to be held in their honor and in that way truly rake in offerings. This is especially true of elder monks. They older they get, the more profit they can make off of birthdays. Therefore, this year I did not even want a birthday celebration. (The Master remained in seclusion at the City of 10,000 Buddhas for the several days surrounding the day of his birthday.) In all we do we have to be different from the common lot. After this, no one is permitted to try and give me a birthday party. If you want to give me a "good birthday" just accrue more merit and virtue. Don't borrow the opportunity to try and make offerings to me personally. I will have none of that.

We are living in the Dharma-ending Age. There is no genuine Dharma. This is not just true of Buddhism, but also of Catholicism, Protestantism, Islam and other religions. Take Catholics, for instance. They used to be real strict and firmly held to the rules. Now, since 1965 the sisters have let their hair grow and they wear lay clothes. Catholicism has gone downhill ever since. Other religions are the same. The founders of those religions never foresaw that their teachings would decline to such an extent. But the Buddha knew. He said long ago, that in the Dharma-ending Age, left home people would wear the Buddha's clothes, eat the Buddha's food, and shit in the Buddha's bowl--thereby destroying Buddhism. The decline of Buddhism is a sign of the Dharma-ending Age. But it affects all other religions as well. It's happening because people's blessings have grown thin. Because there is no one with great blessings anymore, not many sages come into the world, and there is very little Dharma left in the world. In the midst of all this, I don't take account of my own strength, I don't know what I'm trying

to do, but I just keep insisting that the Proper Dharma must
abide in the world. I'm that way, but it's really an exhaust-
ing task. Still, I want to do it. So those of you who follow
me should deeply realize what age it is we are living in.
And you should each ask yourselves, "How can we be outstanding people capable of leading living beings?" Take a good
look at yourself. Do well what you should be doing. Don't
just go along with the crowd. To do that is to be spineless.

* * * * *

ON VIRTUE

Lao Tze said:

> *Those of superior virtue are not attached*
> *   to their virtue.*
> *Those of inferior virtue are attached to*
> *   their virtue.*
> *Those who are attached cannot be said to*
> *   have Way-virtue.*

Those of "superior virtue," cultivate the Bodhisattva Way but are not attached to the traces of practice.
Although they do all kinds of good deeds, they don't have any
trace of doing them.
It's said,

> *Doing good and cultivating virtue is just*
> *   doing what one should be doing.*

You should absolutely not have arrogance or self-
satisfaction in your minds. You shouldn't think,"I am virtuous
and good. I do good deeds."
It's said:

> *Doing good and wanting people to know is*
> *   not true good.*
> *Doing evil and fearing that people will*
> *   find out is truly great evil.*

Those who really cultivate the Bodhisattva Way are not attached to the things they do. They don't become attached to anything. It's not that they have virtue and then become arrogant toward others.

A person with wisdom won't be arrogant and think he has wisdom. A person with Way-virtue won't be arrogant and think he has Way-virtue. A person with scholarship won't be arrogant and think that he has scholarship. A person with cultivation won't be arrogant and think that he has culitvation. Cultivation can't be sold. To genuinely cultivate the Bodhisattva Way you must do what you are supposed to do.

"Inferior virtue" refers to common people who do accomplish a bit of merit and virtue and go everywhere advertising for themselves, "I did this good deed. I did this virtuous act." They cheat people and want people to think well of them. That's just being "an old crook with many transformations." They keep telling people, "At a certain place I built a bridge, made a temple or a stupa, and printed Sutras." If you are attached, then you have no Way-virtue at all. Living beings can't obtain the Way just because of this. It's just because they advertise for themselves. This is a falseness. So it's said,

> Living beings cannot attain the True Way
> Because of falseness.

False thoughts are all falseness: thoughts of killing, thoughts of stealing, thoughts of sexual misconduct, thoughts of false speech, and thoughts of taking intoxicants. Those kinds of false thoughts are really hard to subdue. Why do people cultivate for a long time and still have no response from the Way? It's because of the tricks of false thinking. As soon as you have false thinking, you destroy your samadhi, precept, and wisdom power. If you have false thinking, then your holding of precepts is not solid. If you have false thinking, then your cultivation of samadhi is not solid, not to mention the power of your wisdom! False thoughts are followed by climbing on conditions. Then you run after the ten thousand things. You are turned by them. The states of the ten thousand things are what the eyes see, what the ears hear, what the nose smells, what the tongue tastes, what the body touches and what the mind knows. If you are attached to the ten thousand things and are turned by them, then your mind gives rise to greed and seeking. You will have greed for what you like. Then you will think of ways to get what you like. And you will never get your fill. You can't fill up the bottomless pit. Greed for this, then for that; you are greedy non-stop. Greed for money leads to greed for fame, then for a house, a car, a plane, a yacht, and on and on with no satiation. You are seeking all the time. Sometimes you don't get what you want. Then what? You get afflicted--you get upset. When that happens, all kinds of

false thoughts follow. When the false thoughts come, you
worry and are upset. You suffer in body and mind. When
you eat, the food is without flavor, you can't sleep and your
mind is in agony. You are constantly battling with problems.
Therefore a lot of unclear, unclean actions ensue. A lot of
unclean, filthy, thoughts arise. Because of them you keep
on turning in the cycle of birth and death. The more messed
up you get, the further you get from your self nature, and
you fall into the bitter sea of suffering. Once that happens,
the self-nature's basic substance is as if lost. The basic
substance of the self-nature is the true, permanent Way.
What's that like? It's not like anything you know. If you
understand, you'll obtain the Way. If you fail to understand,
you will fall further and further down day-by-day. If you
can awaken to this principle at all times, the light of your
wisdom will be in evidence. The pure and fundamental wonderful nature of True Suchness will appear.

THE SEVEN EMOTIONS AND TEN INJURIES

Today we'll talk about the Seven Emotions, which are
happiness, rage, grief, fear, love, loathing, and desire.
When these Seven Emotions are used inappropriately, they
have a harmful effect on people. If used correctly, they will
not have a harmful effect, but nonetheless they won't bring any
great benefits either. Therefore cultivators must learn to
control their emotions, and not let emotions run them. As it
is said, "We don't give away the Buddhadharma like a cheap
hand-out in compliance with worldly emotions."
What are the Seven Emotions and how do they harm you?

1. Happiness: If you're too happy, if you experience too
   much elation, that can be harmful to you, because too
   much joy always brings sorrow in the end. Happiness to
   an extreme, is quickly supplanted by grief. Too much
   happiness also hurts the heart; it can give you heart
   trouble.
2. Rage: If you experience too much rage, too much anger,
   then you'll be harmed by it. Of course, a little bit
   won't hurt; but if your anger is too great or you get
   angry too often, then your system cannot take that.
   Too much anger will hurt the liver. You can get a
   liver malady from losing your temper too often.

3. Grief: Sometimes people indulge in excessive grief and cry too much. That can hurt their lungs.
4. Fear: If people experience too much terror, they will be injured by it. Fear hurts the gall bladder.
5. Love: Don't think that love is a good thing. Love really hurts the spirit.
6. Loathing: Loathing means intense dislike. You shouldn't indulge in love, nor should you indulge in loathing. Too much loathing can cause psychological abberations; you can become mentally deranged, crazy.
7. Desire: Desire means excessive craving for anything whatsoever. Too much desire will hurt the spleen.

These Seven Emotions can bring about the seven injurious effects. Therefore cultivators must learn moderation. Confucius put it well, he said:

Before happiness, rage, grief or joy arise, there is the Middle. Should these be tempered by moderation, there is Harmony. The Middle is the basis of heaven and earth. Harmony is the Way that penetrates heaven and earth.

Before any of the Seven Emotions arise, one's mind is in a state of equilibrium--stasis. Should any of these seven notions arise, one should take care that they be tempered by moderation. One should only experience these emotions in the proper amount--not too much, and not too little. In that way, one attains harmony. The Middle Way is the origin, the fundamental of everything in the universe. Harmony is the path that penetrates everything in heaven and earth. Therefore cultivators should take care never to overindulge in the Seven Emotions.

Aside from the Seven Emotions, there are also Ten Kinds of Injuries that cultivators should be aware of. They are:

1. Too much walking injures the sinews: If you walk for a long time without resting, it can injure your sinews, muscles and ligaments.
2. Too much standing injures the bones: On the other hand, if you remain stationary, standing in one place for a very long time, you can in turn injure your bones.
3. Too much sitting injures the blood: This means sitting in a place for a long time without getting up to exercise. However, meditation doesn't fall under this category of sitting. Sitting for a long time can injure your blood.

4. Too much sleeping injures the pulse: You shouldn't think that a lot of sleep is necessarily a good thing, because it can harm your pulse.
5. Too much listening injures one's vitality: If you're always intent on listening to this and listening to that, your energy and vitality get depleted.
6. Too much looking injures the spirit: Too much seeing, for example too much reading is also dangerous. If you read and read and read without stopping, to the point that your eyes get so tired that you can't even pry them open, you're just injuring your spirit.
7. Too much talking injures the breath: As it is said, "Open your mouth and your energy and your breath disperse; wag your tongue and rights and wrongs come forth." So, talking too much can hurt your breath.
8. Too much eating injures the heart: If you over eat, you strain your heart. People who regularly stuff themselves are more prone to get heart diseases for that reason.
9. Too much thinking hurts the spleen: If one is thinking about east, west, north, and south, and one's thoughts just race madly about, then one's spleen will be injured. At that time you lose all appetite for food and nourishment.
10. Too much promiscuity injures the life-force: If people indulge in too much sex they will deplete their very life-force.

For these reasons we can see that there are definite principles which rule our lives, and we can't carry on without any heed for decorum or rules, dissipating our very life-force and energies. We who cultivate the Way must pay special attention to the principles that accord with heaven and earth.

A WORLD INFESTED WITH POISONOUS SNAKES

-Dharma talk by Tripitaka
Master Hsüan Hua
City of 10,000 Buddhas
February 12, 1982

From limitless times past people have had greed, hatred, and stupidity which causes them to create a lot of karmic offenses. And because people don't wish to leave those three poisons behind, the more greedy they are, the more greedy they become; the more hateful they are, the more hateful they become; and the more foolish they are, the more foolish they become. Each day the greed, anger, and foolishness increase, and each day precepts, samadhi, and wisdom decrease. To increase greed, hatred, and foolishness is to increase karmic offenses. And so, as our world becomes filled up with greed, hatred, and delusion; precepts, samadhi, and wisdom disappear without our noticing it. Everyone is attached to greed, hatred, and delusion, and no one cultivates precepts, samadhi, and wisdom. No one holds the precepts. Everybody only knows about killing living beings. Killing karma causes more killing of living beings, to the point that it fills up the heavens. And stealing karma also fills up the heavens. So does the karma of sexual misconduct, false speech, and the taking of intoxicants. Because of this, the hearts of human beings are becoming more and more poisonous every day, and they don't have any compassion. The more poisonous they become, the more greedy they become; the more greedy they become, the more angry they get and the more deluded. Finally, in the end, the whole world will become the World of the Three Poisons.

The World of the Three Poisons could also be called the world of poisonous snakes. Right now every place in the world is filled up with poisonous snakes. These kinds of poisonous snakes have no form. They are invisible. These invisible poisonous snakes exist in every corner of the globe, and they exist within the body of each person. The minds of people are also infested with poisonous snakes. Therefore every person's mind is filled with lethal hatred and anger.

If we want to decrease the amount of our karmic offenses and transgressions, we can't possibly use greed, hatred, and delusion to do it. Instead, we should diligently cultivate precepts, samadhi, and wisdom and eradicate greed, hatred, and delusion. In this way, the world will get better, the human heart will be filled with compassion, and the human mind will be filled with thoughts of Way-karma. This way we can develop wholesome characters. By not creating the karma of killing, stealing, sexual misconduct, false speech, and the taking of intoxicants (including drugs and cigarettes), we can slowly turn the world around and change it. If people's minds do not tend toward the wholesome, then the world will get worse and worse every day. If people's minds tend toward the good, then the world will get better and better every day.

Previously I said that every place in the world is filled with poisonous snakes. You thought I was trying to frighten you, but I wasn't. The whole world IS filled with these snakes! The world is filled with savage, wild animals. One could say that our capability to bring harm to humankind has become even greater than that of savage, wild beasts. You should think this over. Think about how many diseases there are in the world which no medicine can cure. That is a result of the varieties of poisonous hatred that have amassed together. A defiling, resentful energy has appeared, caused by many kinds of strange demons and ghosts.

And so it appears in the world--cause and effect--back and forth, and then comes the retribution. The goblins and ghosts seek for karmic recompense to appease their resentment toward people. I'm not just talking; metaphysically this is truly a world filled with poisonous snakes.

* * * * *

WHEN THE CAUSE-GROUND IS NOT TRUE, THE RESULT WILL BE CROOKED

People who cultivate must actually go ahead and do it. They must intensely cultivate and then they can quickly accomplish the unsurpassed Buddha-fruition. If while cultivating on the causal ground they don't do things truly but are always putting on a false mask and doing things which are phony and untrue, then the result won't be true either. It will be crooked, and there will be no smooth and simple way to accomplish their Way-karma.

The karma we have each created does not begin and end with this one life. It extends back life after life. Our killing karma is limitless and boundless, as is our karma from stealing, lust, lying, and taking intoxicants. We are so confused we are like flies buzzing here and there at random, going nowhere in particular. We have taken numerous wrong turns and made many mistakes. Yet when the time comes to undergo retribution we still won't admit our mistakes. Plant bad causes and you will reap bad effects.

We should be very careful in everything we do. Every mouthful that we eat and drink is already predestined. If in this life people are not good to you, it's because in the past you weren't good to them. If someone scolds you for no reason, it's because in the past you scolded others unreasonably. If someone strikes you without any apparent cause, it's actually because in the past you struck them. We have to pay back all our debts--with interest. Therefore, planting a small bad cause will result in a major bad retribution. But common people don't understand about past causes and future effects and so they curse heaven and blame people for what happens to them. They say that God is not fair and people are unjust.

I often point out to you that this world is totally immersed in fighting. Countries fight with countries, families fight with families, people fight with people, and worlds fight with worlds. All this fighting has its source in killing and hatred. Killing karma fills up the entire universe. Because of it we harm and kill each other. Because of it, many strange diseases manifest which no medicine can cure. Every single person's offenses are limitless and boundless--uncountable. And yet one thinks he or she is fine and doesn't know to deeply repent and reform and truly bring forth the resolve for Bodhi. No one can return the light and look within, no one can exercise self-control. Inside we are always blaming others. Everyone should pay careful attention to this.

When we cultivate we can't be greedy for pleasure. When your desires increase then you are turned upside down. People worry about getting enough nourishment but if you're really cultivating, that's not necessary. It's only when you lose too much of your essential energy that you have to try to build yourself up again. You can lose it in lots of ways. When your eyes look at forms, you lose energy. When your ears listen to pleasing sounds, you lose energy. When your nose greedily smells fragrances, you lose energy. When your tongue tastes good flavors, you lose energy--your essence. When your body enjoys tactile contact, you lose energy. And when your mind gets involved in conditioned dharmas you lose energy. In all these ways you lose your essence. You have outflows. You can't look after yourself when it comes to these subtle aspects but instead roll around in ignorance and spin into afflictions.

This is especially important for left-home people to be attentive to. Is it that you can't take a loss? You can't put it all down, can't take the suffering? Most especially left-home people shouldn't enjoy pleasures and do things to help out their stinking skin bags. You should be aware that when your time comes to die, your body won't give you so much as a "thank you." It won't be like that. It's just a mass of flesh and bones--a false combination of the four elements. It's not true. The self-nature is what's true. It is penetratingly bright and dazzling with light. The self-nature is described in the lines:

*Originally there's not one thing,
So where can the dust alight?*

Go inside. Don't spin on the surface. Don't always be thinking about what's good for you. You should not have a self. No mark of self, others, living beings, or a life-span. Don't always be calculating about how to avoid hunger and cold.

If you can't see through it and put it all down, then you cannot obtain self mastery. When you hear this, you may not think it seems like much, but if you do it, you will have success. You must use a true mind to cultivate. You can't be sloppy. Cultivators should always be willing to take a loss and should not look for bargains. You should be good to others and not worry about yourself. You absolutely can't ever be jealous and you absolutely can't be without merit and virtue. If you have the tiniest bit of selfishness, or self benefit, you can't get genuine wisdom. If you begin by being selfish, you will just end up selfish. When you cultivate you cannot fear suffering, difficulty, or lack of money.

I remember when I left Manchuria and went to the internal provinces, I had just a little bit of money with me--just enough to get me to P'u T'ou Mountain to take the Precepts.

At T'ien Jin I went to pay my respects to Dharma Master T'an Hsü and D.M. Ding Hsi, because they were the Great Virtuous Elders in Manchuria. All I wanted to do was bow to them but when they saw this young novice, they thought I'd come to try to beg from them. So. D.M. Ding Hsi said, "Whatever it is you want, go see the Abbot. I don't watch over others affairs." D.M. T'an Hsü said the same thing, and when I took a look at the Abbot, I saw he was yet another person who just looked at the ceiling when anyone tried to talk to him. This really made me sad. Greatly virtuous ones should take care not to look lightly on those who come to study with them.

Then I heard that D.M. T'i Jing and a following of ten bhikshus and novices--all of whom studied with him--were going to Hu Bei, so I joined with them to travel. But then D.M. T'i Jing announced, "You all have to turn over all your money to me as head of this party. No one is allowed to have any private holdings."

So I gave him my P'u T'ou Mountain money and travelled with them to Hu Bei. It was cold--snowing--and I only wore three lays of clothes and no padded clothing. The clothes I did have were tattered, but at that time my "state" was good. I had no thoughts. So every day a rare fragrance permeated and surrounded me. It was not like incense--it was a fragrance not of this world. The same thing used to happen in Manchuria, too. I think it was a response from cultivating ascetic practices. The Buddhas and Bodhisattvas were happy and the heavenly maidens scattered flowers. At that time, the states which occurred were special like that.

The following year (1947), I went to P'u T'ou Mountain to receive the Precepts. But when I asked D.M. T'i Jing for my P'u T'ou Mountain money back, he said, "Not a penny. You can't go. This monastery is transmitting the Precepts. Take them here."

I said, "My vow is to go to P'u T'ou. If I don't go, I'll not fulfill my vow. If you won't give me my money, I'll go without it."

So that's what I did. I got a free boat. The food was free and I slept on the deck. I went to Ning Bwo, Shen Jia Men, to P'u T'ou Mountain to take Precepts. At P'u T'ou, it was very convenient because one didn't need money to receive the Precepts. When I came down from the mountain, I got a boat to Shanghai--somehow the money worked out for it without my really knowing how. I went to Su Chou to Ling Yen Mountain to study the Sutra teachings at the Buddhist Academy. I had thirty classmates and to them I appeared to be really dumb. They all looked down on me because I didn't talk, I didn't develop relationships or make friends. It was bitter like that for several decades. Then I went to Hong Kong for ten years and then came to America. But I had no plans then, and I don't have any now--no calculations.

Now there is the City of Ten Thousand Buddhas and I still don't make plans. I just don't think about it. I just go forward and do what I can. I'm really a person "whose past mind cannot be got at, whose present mind cannot be got at, and whose future mind cannot be got at." So this confused person came to America and now there is the City of Ten Thousand Buddhas and everyday we are building and improving it. I'm a person without any scholastic learning and I have no Way-virtue and no wisdom. I'm just a plain, dumb person, but I'm diligent and responsible about what I do. I pay no attention to whether you believe in me or not. I just go forward step-by-step and do what I can for Buddhism. That is my principle.

If people who have left home cannot truly cultivate, there's no use in leaving home.

If you yourself cultivate, you can end your own birth and death.
If you yourself eat, you will get full.

Anyone who cultivates can have a share in this. If you don't cultivate, not only will I not be able to save you, even the Buddha can't save you.
   If you don't cultivate and just cheat others, you will fall into the hells. You have to be extremely careful and very diligent and not the least bit casual. If those who are within Buddhism don't do things truly, who in this world will?
   You all have eyes and can see what I do here every day. Don't look every day and still not understand and keep on creating offenses. If you're like this, you can't be helped.
   Those who live at the City of Ten Thousand Buddhas should bring forth a true mind for Bodhi. Don't be muddled, harbor selfishness, or seek for self-benefit.

* * * * *

LIFE AT THE CITY OF TEN THOUSAND BUDDHAS

   There are some people at the City of Ten Thousand Buddhas who truly want to cultivate the Way, so that at all times they return the light and look within, they check out their minds and bodies to be sure they are not breaking the Five Precepts of,
   No killing
   No stealing
   No false speech
   No sexual misconduct
   No intoxicants

At all times they exercise caution and are attentive and sincere in their cultivation. For example, the monks who practice Three Steps One Bow look after themselves at all times and don't want to have false thinking. Granted, they still have false thinking sometimes, but they are able to recognize those false thoughts and they know that it's wrong to have them and are able to pull them back. Then,

> When one thought arises one awakens to it,
> Once awakened to, it is gone.

Trace the source of your false thoughts. For example, if you have false thoughts of eating food, it's because you are a gluttonous person. If you have false thoughts about sounds, it is because you are greedy to listen to fine sounds. If you have false thoughts about sights you see, it's because you enjoy indulging in visual forms. If you have false thoughts about bodily contact, it is because you are greedy to experience sensual pleasures. If you have false thoughts about ideas and concepts, it means you are prone to seeking mental dharmas.

If you are like that, then it means you haven't made it through those gates. You run out the six gates of eyes, ears, nose, tongue, body and mind. The six sense organs get confused by the six sense objects. But the six sense organs can "turn" the six sense objects. When that can be done then you are capable of "not entering" the gates. The Six sense objects are:

> forms
> sounds
> smells
> tastes
> objects of touch, and
> dharmas

When you have passed through the gates, fame and profit won't move you either. You are then not influenced by anything:

> The eyes see shapes and forms, but inside there is nothing.
> The ears hear defiling sounds, but the mind does not know.

You are no longer turned by false aspects of your environment. But even at that point you must use effort and advance. You can't slack off, because if you do, the old bad habits will appear again. Not everyone who is here is making a genuine effort. Only some people are.

There are others here who just follow the crowd. They see others reciting the Buddha's name, so they do too, but they don't understand why they are doing it. There are also those who make a practice of reading Sutras or reciting mantras, but it's as if they were just swallowing a

date whole without knowing the flavor. Some of these
people get to the point that even though they live in the
Bodhimanda, they create offenses. They violate the Five
Precepts: killing, stealing, sexual misconduct, false
speech, taking intoxicants, which means they smoke, drink,
or take dope. There are even those who have left home
within the Bodhimanda whose minds are filthy. So what can
you do to change this situation? Increase your virtuous
practices and then offenses will gradually disappear. How
can you increase your merit and virtue? Just by taking a
loss. By not looking for bargains. In a Bodhimanda you
should always renounce yourself for the sake of others and
subdue yourself according to principle. With an attitude
like that, you will not be wasting your time while living
in the Bodhimanda.

    To repent and reform again and again before the assembly is not the way. Repentance and reform means you don't
commit those offenses again. You can't keep committing
them and repenting thinking that you are cleansed each
time. That is just showing disrespect for the Dharma of
repentance and reform. You can't just tell everyone about
the offenses you've committed figuring that that will cause
them to disappear. Such an approach is very dangerous. If
you keep committing them, you'll eventually end up in the
unintermittent hells. I am obliged to tell you that I'm
not just here to entertain you and play games.

* * * * *

*Just as the Russian River
flows every day;
At the City of Ten Thousand Buddhas,
the Dharma is lectured every day.*

    Some people work hard every day. Some come here to
the City of Ten Thousand Buddhas, but their virtuous conduct is not sufficient because they have not planted enough
good roots. So when they come to the City of Ten Thousand
Buddhas they are false-thinking all the time, thinking that
the City of Ten Thousand Buddhas is too much suffering.
Left-home people eat only one meal a day here, and although
lay people may eat more often, the food is very simple and
plain. The schedule is so tight and full that even if they
wanted to be lazy, it would be embarrassing for them. They
might want to goof off a little, but they don't think they
can get away with it, so they can't live here.

The City of Ten Thousand Buddhas is a Bodhimanda in the West where the Proper Dharma is constantly turning. We cultivate non-stop through wind and rain and snow and cold. People with a mind for the Way come here, and this is where they want to stay. People with no Way-mind find it totally uncomfortable every minute here. Some think it's good, some don't, yet this place remains the same. In this world people's faces, thoughts, and actions are all different. One person likes it one way, and another person likes it another. It's complex and inconceivable. At the City of Ten Thousand Buddhas we bear bitterness and endure toil. We want to truly bring forth the Bodhi mind, cultivate, and be faithful disciples of the Buddha. But those who don't have enough good roots sooner or later will leave. They may force it when they first come, but eventually they will go because the City of Ten Thousand Buddhas is not convenient and comfortable. Every day we toil and suffer-- we forget ourselves for the sake of the Dharma. And now every evening there is an AVATAMSAKA Assembly where the Sutra is lectured. This is a point that everyone should deeply investigate.

Some come to the City of Ten Thousand Buddhas and for them it's like coming home. They don't want to leave. Heng Tao's father said, "No matter how bad a person has been, when he comes to the City of Ten Thousand Buddhas, he has to be good." For a person so experienced in the ways of the world to come up with an opinion like that is not a simple matter.

Some come to the City of Ten Thousand Buddhas saying that they are cultivators, but they can't digest it. Their bodies can't take it. They can't bear the City of Ten Thousand Buddhas, so they can't live here. Some want to live here but circumstances prevent it: their livelihood, immigration problems, illness, and so on. Some truly want to live here like D.M. Chiuo Kan from Japan. He's been here for six months this time and was really happy. But his back hurts so he has to go back to Japan. I had arranged with him that he would lecture today, but he couldn't wait. So he left on March 30th or 31st. Too bad.

True cultivators want to stay here, and yet sometimes they just can't. So people who don't want to cultivate <u>absolutely can't</u> stay. The City of Ten Thousand Buddhas is the True Dharma dwelling in the world. One Korean monk came and said he wanted to stay here--to live out his entire life here. But eventually he went back to Korea and now he can't return because of immigration problems.

Cultivation is really not easy. And it's really not easy to find a place where people work hard and cultivate the Way. In the future many left-home and lay people from other countries will come here.

If a person is a City of Ten Thousand Buddhas person, even if the people here were to agree to kick him out, he still wouldn't leave. If he's not a City of Ten Thousand Buddhas person, he won't stay no matter what you do for him. Everything has its own causes and conditions.

* * * * *

ALL FROM A SINGLE THOUGHT

People in the world are born as if drunk and die as if in a dream. They don't know how to get out of the pain of the turning wheel of rebirth. They've been doing it from of old: dying and getting reborn, then dying again. It's like putting on a play. In this play, you're an emperor; in the next play you find yourself a beggar. When you're an emperor, you don't remember the difficulty of being a beggar; when you're a beggar you don't remember the pleasures of the palace. You don't remember from one lifetime to the next. But how many offenses have you created? How much virtue have you fostered? You don't know. You are trying to seek escape from ignorance. But the more you seek the Way, the farther into darkness you go, and the farther from the Path you get. What should you do? You get on the wrong road because your false mind plays tricks on you. You don't seek within your true mind--within your wisdom. Ignorance, or lack of light, is a lack of wisdom. Without wisdom, everything you do is upside down. You take right for wrong and wrong for right. Even though you clearly know that something is right, you don't do it. But when you clearly know that something is wrong, you go ahead and do it anyway. You mistakenly enter the wrong path and never find the Proper Way.

We who study the Buddhadharma want to smash through ignorance and reveal the Dharma nature. When you're obstructed by ignorance you like to do messed-up things and don't like to do clear, bright things. You have deviant knowledge and deviant views. Selfishness takes over, and you are not open and public-minded, with straight, proper, and unbiased views. Because of this, you fall farther and farther in life after life. Each life you are worse than you were before--down, down until eventually you become a mosquito or an ant with only a bit of awareness left, and still you're insatiably greedy and do muddled things. Take a look at creatures--they all have their own particular natures. Basically they all have the Buddha-nature, but their natures disperse and their souls scatter so they become truly dumb--not at all bright and aware. People are the most intelligent of all creatures, but the greatest offenses are created in the human realm. So there's a verse that describes the Chinese character for mind (hsin 心):

> *Three dots like a cluster of stars;*
> *And a hook like a crescent moon.*
> *Animals come from this;*
> *And Buddhas are made from it too.*

If in your mind you do dog things, you'll become a dog. It's the same if you do chicken things in your mind. If you do sheep things in your mind, you'll become a sheep, if you do horse things you'll become a horse, cow things you'll become a cow. Becoming a Buddha or a Patriarch also comes from the mind.

> *Everything is made from the mind alone.*

The suffering in the hells and the pleasures of the heavens all come from a single thought of the mind.

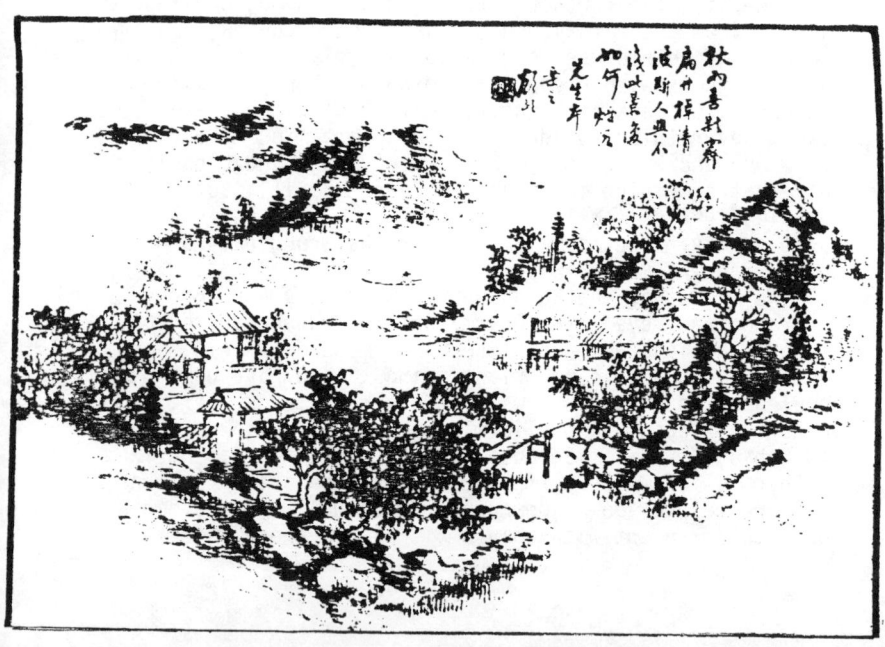

DON'T SELL YOUR CULTIVATION

It's said,

> *The paths of good and evil are two different roads.*
> *Those who cultivate, cultivate, and those who create evil, create evil.*

What does it mean to cultivate? Here it refers to cultivating precepts, samadhi, and wisdom and wholesome merit and virtue. To walk the other path means to create evil deeds, to involve oneself in greed, hatred, and stupidity. Wholesome merit and virtue are derived from holding the five precepts and doing the ten good deeds. Merit means outside, establishing good deeds. Virtue means inside, constantly fortifying oneself with wisdom. Therefore, a cultivator must make it his business to cultivate precepts, samadhi, and wisdom. Many Buddhists hear these terms over and over again, and yet those who actually practice according to them are very, very few. Praising oneself and disparaging others is a really common sickness among Buddhists. It is a common durge of humankind. Everyone wants to be number one; everyone wants to be recognized as an outstanding person, a living Buddha, a Patriarch, or a living Bodhisattva. How do they get to be living Buddhas, living Bodhisattvas, and living Patriarchs? They do it by bragging about their merit and virtue. They advertise for themselves and put the other guy down so that it looks like they are the only outstanding persons in the entire world.

Sometimes people clearly know that they are not up to others, but they still don't admit it to themselves. They still make it look like they are "out of sight" and would never think of divulging their own short-comings, but only brag about their own long points. This is to praise oneself and disparage others; this is not in accord with the Precepts, but in opposition to the Way. How does one accord with the Precepts? In every movement one is always mindful of oneself. True cultivators guard their mouths at all times. They plug them up as if plugging up a bottle, so as to not to commit one of the four evils of the tongue.

> *When dwelling with a group of people,*
> *guard your tongue.*
> *When staying alone by yourself,*
> *watch over your own heart.*

You should watch over your own thoughts. If you have thoughts that you are someone special and extraordinary, you're just giving rise to arrogance. By doing that you leave yourself open for a deviant demon to enter your heart. Once that happens to you, you give rise to deviant knowledge and views and to an impure and insane kind of wisdom. You will become a glib talker, to the point that even if you know you are wrong, you will still distort the situation so that you come out on top. You will be able to rationalize anything to make yourself sound good.

And so you ask me, "Dharma Master, have you violated this precept?" Honestly, I will tell you that I have violated this precept. In my younger days, I got a bit of accomplishment within the Buddhadharma and I went everywhere showing off my skills. I didn't blatantly praise myself and disparage others, but I exhibited my cultivation by only wearing three layers of cotton, padded clothing, no matter whether it was summer or winter. In Manchuria, the winters got so cold it went to 38 degrees below zero. People can die from that kind of weather, even if they wear fur clothing.

The cold was so bitter that it felt like knives cutting into your face. But even during those times I "sold" my cultivation and wore only three layers of cotton clothing. I also wore no shoes but walked barefoot on the snow. I never talked about my cultivation, but I showed off.

And so a lot of ignorant people were deceived by me. They were so awed, that whenever they saw me they would bow down in the streets and say, "Living Bodhisattva, you really have some skill." Even those of outside ways were impressed and expressed reverence. But I engaged in cheap games. Looking back on it, I see it was just demonic karma. Even though I was impervious to the heat and cold, was it necessary for me to make a show of it? Although I didn't talk about it, nonetheless, I caused other cultivators who had not reached my level of practice to look bad and that was, in effect, disparaging others and praising oneself.

There were a few other Dharma Masters who said, "Your cultivation isn't so remarkable; consider the sparrows, they walk on the snow without any shoes and socks, and yet they don't have any cultivation." What those people said really had principle to it. Although their tone was somewhat sour, it did help me to break through those attachments.

And then there was the business of eating only one meal a day. Basically, I didn't have to show off and advertise in that way, either. But I made mistakes when I was young. Now I have changed. Nowadays I wear more clothing when it's cold. I was sixteen or seventeen when I began the practice

of eating only one meal a day--I hadn't even left the home-
life. People thought I was a real weirdo. Now I wear as
many clothes as other people do--even more. And I don't go
around bragging that I only eat one meal a day. It's only
in the past few years that I have come to a bit of understanding about cultivation. I no longer have to make a big
to-do or advertise or engage in false speech by depracating
others and praising myself.

This year I am going on seventy, and I realize the mistakes of my past sixty-nine years. In the past I was really
conceited and brash, and so it is a fitting retribution that
people bad-mouth me nowadays. They are my good knowing
advisors, causing me to repent and reform. If they didn't
see faults in me, they wouldn't be saying such things. Now
I am telling you about my past practices of deviant knowledge
and views. In the past I used tricks to bewilder people,
cashed in on sensationalism and influenced them to think I
was tops. But today, I am apologizing to all of you. I don't
want to mislead those of you who have taken refuge with me.

*Follow what is good and retreat from what
is bad.
If it accords with the Way, progress along
with it,
But if it isn't the Way, turn back from it.*

I myself have walked on the wrong road, but I don't want you
to walk on the same road again and make the same mistakes.
I am telling you this, but whether or not you listen is up
to you.

THE TEN DHARMA REALMS
ARE NOT BEYOND A SINGLE THOUGHT

All the subtle secrets of the universe are not beyond a single thought in living beings' minds. Whether it's science, philosophy, or any other branch of learning--none goes beyond the human mind. Each living being within the Ten Dharma Realms does his own job. Buddhas do the work of Buddhas. Actually Buddhas don't have to do anything, because they've accomplished everything they set about to do. However, if Buddhas didn't do anything, they wouldn't be able to save living beings, in which case they wouldn't be Buddhas, therefore they do Buddha deeds. Meanwhile, Bodhisattvas do the work of Bodhisattvas, Sound Hearers do the work of Sound Hearers, and those Enlightened to Conditions do the work of those Enlightened to Conditions. The gods do the work of gods. Basically there's nothing for them to do, but after they have eaten their fill, they just toodle around minding others' business. So, everyone within the universe does his or her own job. If one doesn't do anything, then when alive one is a lazy person, and when dead one is a lazy ghost.

Now why do Buddhas and Bodhisattvas mind other people's business? Bodhisattvas still have one section of production-mark ignorance which they haven't broken through;consequently they still have a tiny trace of attachment which they have not completely put down. Buddhas of course, have broken through all ignorance and attachment, and therefore they do without doing; they are completely without attachment. Among gods, there are many who haven't broken through view delusions, thought delusions and delusions like dust and sand--the three types of delusions. Only when one attains to the first fruit of Arhatship does one cut off view delusions. At this time one is impervious to both external and internal states. One is no longer moved by situations.

What is meant by view delusions? They are what arise when "upon seeing a state, one begets greed and love." As long as a state doesn't arise, one is not confused; but once a state arises, one brings forth greed and fondness for it, and hence becomes confused. There are eighty-one grades of view delusions.

What is meant by thought delusions? They are what arise when "confused about principles, one gives rise to discrimination." One is unclear about principles, and gives rise to false discrimination. Arhats of the second and third fruition have completely cut off thought delusions, of which there are eighty-eight.

And what is meant by delusions like dust and sand? These are the most subtle kind of delusion--as subtle as tiny motes

of dust or grains of sand, but they occlude your true wisdom
and nature all the same. There are nine grades of delusion
like dust and sand. Arhats of the fourth fruition have severed
this type of delusion. Because of this they,

> *Transcend the Triple Realm*
> *and are no longer trapped within the five elements.*

"*Triple Realm*" refers to the desire realm, form realm and
formless realm. Living beings within the desire realm still
have desire--greed and lust. Living beings within the form
realm do not have such heavy desire; however they still have a
physical form and appearance. They are still attached to
appearances and therefore they are not apart from the marks of
self, others, living beings, and lifespans. Living beings in
the formless realm are without form or shape, yet they still
have consciousness and they are attached to this consciousness.
The formless realm includes the Heaven of Unbounded Emptiness,
the Heaven of Unbounded Consciousness, the Heaven of Nothing
Whatsoever, and the Heaven of Neither Thought nor Non-Thought
--the Four Heavens of Boundlessness.

Because living beings within these three realms are still
attached, they cannot get out. Only those who are certified to
the fourth fruition of Arhatship can completely escape. But
Arhats still belong to the Lesser Vehicle; only Bodhisattvas
belong to the Great Vehicle. Now make sure you don't go around
advertising yourself as a Bodhisattva. Bodhisattvas are without
attachment to food, sleep and clothes. Can you go without food,
sleep, and clothes? If you cannot, then you're still not a
Bodhisattva.

When an Arhat of the first fruition walks, his feet do not
touch the ground. His feet are about one tenth of a centimeter
above ground level, and in that way, he doesn't kill any tiny
insects or bugs. Can you do that? If you can't then you're
still not an Arhat.

Gods can also walk and travel about in empty space without
any impediment. However, they haven't certified to Arhatship.
It's because they are endowed with the Five Spiritual Penetrations that they are capable of astral travel and other spiritual
feats. Gods do not have physical form like we human beings do.
They are etherical spiritual beings who have magical energy and
are invisible to most people's flesh eyes.

As for Asuras, they're really ugly--grotesque! Some of
them have human heads and animal bodies, some have animal heads
and human bodies. Some have three heads and six arms, or seven
hands and eight feet. Most of them are half-beast and half-
human. Anyway, if you took one look at them you'd be terrified
to death.

What about humans? There are also infinite varieties
within the human species. There are those of the yellow race,
the white race, the red race, the black race, and so forth.
Moreover, within each of those different races, there are
many sub-variations. The *Avatamsaka Sutra* puts it this way:

> *If one wishes to know*
> *All Buddhas of the three periods of time,*
> *One should contemplate the Dharma Realm:*
> *Everything is made from mind alone.*

Living beings of the nine Dharma Realms combine to create
this universe. Whether our world is a good place or bad place
is something that directly relates to every living creature
within the nine Dharma Realms. Everyone's got a responsibi-
lity--a share of the work. However, people's thoughts are
all different. Just take the City of 10,000 Buddhas. For example, there are those among you who really want to cultivate.
But there are also those who do not wish to cultivate, who
are faking it or trying to get some advantage from this place.
Isn't that strange? We're all people, yet some of us want
to create merit and virtue, while others are bent upon creating karmic offenses.

All living beings have different behavior, different
thought patterns, and different appearances. It's so wonderful that it's wonderful beyond words. Someone may say
that human beings are the stupidest category among the beings of the nine Dharma Realms. But animals are even more
stupid than human beings. Human beings may be prone to be
very stupid, but on the other hand, they can also be said to
be very clever. They all go down the same road, yet while
travelling on it, some create merit and virtue, while others
create offenses.

The ancients put it well. They said this of the character for "mind" (*hsin* 心):

> *Three dots like a cluster of stars;*
> *And a hook like a crescent moon.*
> *Animals come from this;*
> *And Buddhas are made from it too.*

Everything is made from the mind alone.

As for the rest of the Dharma Realms: animals are really dumb. All they know is how to eat all day long. Hungry
ghosts are full of hatred; they always feel that others aren't
being good to them. As for hell-beings, well, they're the
worst off, for their sufferings know no bounds. And yet the
Ten Dharma Realms are not apart from a single thought.

Over ten years ago I wrote a little book of verses, titled
The Ten Dharma Realms Are Not Beyond a Single Thought. Over

all these years it seems to me that none of you have paid attention to the principles set forth in that little book, but I've never said anything. However, the time must be right now, for recently I received a letter from a god, and he seems to recognize me somewhat. This heavenly being wrote to me via an earthly medium--his "scribe".

There's nothing unusual about heavenly beings like him travelling around in what we call UFO's and commanding a certain amount of spiritual powers.

Right now the demon kings throughout the trichiliocosm are all aiming at the City of 10,000 Buddhas, ready to attack at anytime. Anyone among you who is heedless and doesn't cultivate, will easily be captured and carried away to become part of the demonic retinue. Just now I said that Buddhas wish that all living beings will become good and wholesome. But strangely enough, living beings seem to want to do just the opposite. They specialize in creating evil. So, there are some of you who continue to be greedy, contentious, full of seeking, selfish and seeking self-benefit. Wouldn't you say that is pitiful? No wonder Lao Tze said,

Everyone knows the beautiful as beautiful
but they indulge in evil instead.
Everyone knows the good as good
but they do what is unwholesome instead.

He wasn't off by a hair in his remark.

* * * * *

ZERO

FROM BEGINNINGLESS TIME ONWARD, LIVING BEINGS HAVE LONG REVOLVED IN BIRTH AND DEATH. There is no beginning nor will there be an end to the time they have revolved and will revolve in birth and death in the six paths. Throughout all time living beings have and still are spinning and will continue to spin back and forth, going around and around the wheel of birth and death. They are just like motes of dust --suddenly in the heavens, suddenly on the ground, suddenly they are in the paths of people, suddenly in the paths of hungry ghosts, suddenly they become animals, suddenly they fall into the hells, and all of a sudden they're asuras. This is what's meant by "no time when it begins and no time when it ends." At whatever time you are able to certify to the fruit and accomplish Buddhahood--at that point--you will be able to

stop the wheel of birth and death. But before you become a
Buddha, you are still turning on the revolving wheel. Even
Bodhisattvas experience delusion during transmigration and
moving in a "skandha" body, and Arhats become confused from
dwelling in the womb. So, even when great lords of the Dharma
body, appear in the human world, sometimes they find themselves
caught up in the flow of birth and death to the extent that
their brains are addled and their heads are bewildered and
they don't know how they can cut off the flow of birth and
death. Birth and death means being born and dying, dying and
being born again. You can speak of major births and deaths,
but there are also minor births and deaths. On the day that
you are born, although there's birth, there's also a kind of
death. Because on the day that you're born, you bring along
with you, the day of your death. This life that we live is
a major "birth and death," and every single thought that goes
by is a minor death. The day that we're born is also the day
we die. Because when there is birth there is also death, and
if there were no births, there would also be no deaths.

Speaking about the word "beginningless", most people
would explain it to mean having no start and no end. "Without
a beginning" means the time from beginningless kalpas in the
past. There's no beginning to kalpas and no end to kalpas.
But if you were to talk about it exhaustively, back and forth,
what does it mean exactly? What does "having no beginning and
no end" mean? It's what we call "0" --a zero. In Chinese, it's
called a "ling"(零). This Zero has no beginning and no end.
There's no point where it starts and no point where it ends.
It's a complete, round circle and it represents the beginningless and endless. The beginningless is represented by the
Zero. If you break up this Zero, it becomes a One, and <u>that</u>
is called a beginning.

Last night I told each of you to pay special attention
to this passage, and today I'm going to tell you about the
Zero, which is very important. Once you cut it open, there's
a One--that which is a beginning. Add another One to it and
you have two. Add another One to it and you've got three.
Add another One and you've got four, then five, six, seven,
eight, nine, and ten. Once there are ten, it multiplies into
one-hundred, and one-hundred multiplies into one-thousand,
and a thousand multiplies into ten thousand, a hundred thousand, a million, a billion, ten billion, up to a figure that
can't even be reckoned. Now in this Scientific Age, we've made
rockets which orbit in space. They can orbit around in space
without ever stopping. This is a product of those numbers.
The beginning of numbers makes it possible for rockets to
venture out into space. The transformations and changes of
numbers mark the beginning.

Well, what about the end? Right now we don't know when
the end will be. The end refers to the fourth of the four
stages of: formation, existence, decay, and emptiness. The
end refers to the period of going empty. Right now we are
in the beginning. There are twenty small kalpas of formation,
twenty small kalpas of existing, twenty small kalpas of decay,
and twenty small kalpas of emptiness. You could speak of this
in terms of a beginning and an end. So now we are speaking of
all living beings from beginningless time onwards. Where do
all these living beings come from? Let's investigate it.
Let's talk about the human race. Would you say men came
first or women came first? If you say men came first, how
did they get here without any women? And if you say women
came first, how could there be women if there weren't any men?
This is also the beginningless because no one knows where it
began.

You can also talk about chickens. Which came first, the
chicken or the egg? From beginningless kalpas onward, there
were no chickens. Where did they come from? They came from
eggs. Now if there were no chickens, how could there be eggs?
So this isn't something you can solve with research. This
principle is just a principle of the beginningless. People
also came from this no-beginning, from this Zero. Because
they came from this zero, there's no beginning, no end, no
inside, no outside, no big, and no small. In terms of the
small, this Zero represents a small mote of dust, an atom.
If you speak about it in larger terms, it includes the entire
Dharma Realm. To the end of space and pervading the Dharma
Realm, nothing gets left outside of the Zero. If you pound
up the whole Dharma Realm which extends up to the end of
space into fine motes of dust--into the tiniest motes of
dust--nothing is left outside of the Zero.

So this Zero is the source of all creation. It has no
beginning and no end. It's the principle of True Emptiness
and Wonderful Existence. The Zero, if spoken of in large
terms, includes all of space and the Dharma Realm. This is
True Emptiness. If you shrink it way down, it turns into a
single atom. And although these atoms are small, they make
up Wonderful Existence. The Zero is True Emptiness and
Wonderful Existence. All of you should think this over. If
you want to understand this doctrine, you have to understand
the true Dharma. If you don't understand this doctrine, then
you're still a confused, muddled person and you have no real
wisdom. If you're enlightened, the Zero is a great, bright,
wisdom light. If you haven't become enlightened, then it is
a state of non-brightness--there is no light. In other words,
it's ignorance. This ignorance is also the Zero. Wisdom light
also makes up the Zero. The Zero is beginningless, endless;

it has no inside, no outside; it is neither small nor large.
The Zero is so large that nothing is left outside of it. You
can draw it as large as you like and if you want to shrink
it down, you can shrink it down as small as you want. It's
so big there's nothing outside of it, and so small you can't
fit anything inside it. If you draw it really large, then
it is the pure basic source of the Wonderful Suchness nature.
If you shrink it way down, make it very, very small, it
becomes your very first thought of ignorance. So when I
speak of the "beginningless" this is what I mean.

Living beings "have long revolved in birth and death."
In the six paths of rebirth, the revolving wheel is included
in the Zero. Not being able to smash through the Zero, one
is born and dies, dies and then is born again. And nobody
knows for how many great kalpas one turns in the six paths.
This is called turning in the six paths of birth and death
for a long time. Isn't this really terrifying--turning
around and around in the revolving wheel?

I'll present another topic to you. This turning for
a long time refers to what you have created through your
continual thought processes. If you produce a defiled
thought, then when that thought matures, you may become an
animal, a hungry ghost or a hell dweller. However, if you
become just a little bit good, you can be born as a human
being or an asura, or perhaps get born in the heavens.
These different paths of rebirth all come about from thoughts.
The revolving wheel is created by your thoughts alone. We
undergo the retribution of being born in the six paths
because of the karma which our thoughts created. It's not
that we receive the retribution immediately, but say if in
the distant past you had false thoughts about the heavens,
then you were born in the heavens. If you had false thoughts
about asuras, then you became an asura. If you had false
thoughts about human beings, then you became a human being.
Or if you had false thoughts of animals, you became an animal.
Having hungry ghosts thoughts, you became a hungry ghost.
Having hellish thoughts, you fell into the hells. If you
mainly did offensive things and created evil karma, then you
fell into the three evil paths. If you did good things which
gained merit and virtue, you were born in the three good
paths. This is speaking in very general terms. If one were
to speak of it in detail one couldn't finish explaining it
until the end of time. So the world is the creation of
false thinking of living beings. If people didn't have
false thinking, the whole world would be empty.

But living beings continue to get born and die, "not
understanding the true and actual Dharma." Living beings
fail to understand the principle of the Dharma of True

Emptiness and Wonderful Existence--the Real Mark of True Suchness, which is the true and actual Dharma. The Dharma of True Emptiness and Wonderful Existence is what I have just explained as the Zero. It is through the Zero that this huge heaven and huge earth were created. And this huge world was also born from the Zero. The myriad living beings also came out of the Zero. Everything has come forth from the Zero. This is because the Zero is not included in numbers-- it transcends numbers. It has no beginning, no end, nothing inside of it, nor outside of it; it's neither big, nor small. If you let it go, it expands to fill the entire universe-- all of creation. If you shrink it down, then it hides away; it would seem to disappear. This Dharma is just the Dharma of True Emptiness and Wonderful Existence.

True Emptiness is not empty. Why isn't it empty? Because it has Wonderful Existence. And Wonderful Existence is not existence. Why is it not existence? Because it still has True Emptiness. True Emptiness doesn't obstruct Wonderful Existence, and Wonderful Existence doesn't obstruct True Emptiness. This principle solves the problem of "which came first, the men or the women?" It also solves the problem of "which came first, the chicken or the egg?" In fact, all of the questions can be solved by using the Zero.

Why is this? The Zero *is* True Emptiness. And within True Emptiness, Wonderful Existence manifests. All creation can manifest. Although there is Wonderful Existence, it is not separate from True Emptiness. If you haven't attained the Mind-Seal Dharma of all Buddhas, you won't be able to understand this. If you understand the "using the mind to seal the mind" Dharma of all Buddhas, then you'll understand this Dharma. So it says, "not understanding the true and actual Dharma." Living beings put a head on top of a head; they run around on a donkey looking for a donkey; they look outside, grasping outwardly, and they don't know how to return the light and reverse the illumination, to recognize the true and actual Dharma inherent within their original self-nature. They don't know that it is forever complete within their own self-nature, that they don't have to go out looking for it. If you look outside, you can look for 84,000 kalpas but you'll never find it. But if you can return the light and reverse the illumination, then you'll immediately realize it. So it says,

The sea of suffering is boundless,
But a turn of the head is the other shore.

This means, if you look outside, the sea of suffering is boundless. But if you turn around and look inside, if you look in your own self-nature, then, that is "to turn your head and arrive at the other shore."

Because living beings don't understand the true and actual Dharma, ALL BUDDHAS COME INTO THE WORLD. We living beings are so upside-down and confused. All day long we seek after false conditions. We get caught up in the six sense organs and the six sense objects and run after them. Originally all Buddhas abide in the Pure Land of Constant, Stillness and Light, sitting in full lotus and rapt in samadhi. But now they enter the world. Why is this? Because they see that you and I--all these stupid creatures--are really pitiful! All day long we forget about what is true and all we know how to do is to get attached to what is false. People don't know to turn away from their confusion and head for enlightenment; to turn away from the false and head for the true; to borrow what is false in order to cultivate what is true;to turn around and look for it inside. This is really pitiful. So, all Buddhas, in their samadhi, produce a mind of great compassion and come into the world to show living beings how to get out of the path of confusion. But we people get caught up pursuing false conditions and don't recognize the true Dharma. The Buddha speaks the Dharma for us and the more the Buddha speaks, the more we try to run away. We try to turn back; we don't listen. The Buddha gets so nervous he starts shaking his head! What are we going to do? We turn around and come back, the Buddha is right in front of our faces! And he teaches us again.

ALL DHARMAS ARE INDESTRUCTIBLE. True and actual Dharma cannot be destroyed by any outside ways. NOR IS THERE ANYONE WHO CAN DESTROY THEM. If you understand and recognize this true and actual Dharma, then you are included in this real Dharma which exhausts the Dharma Realm and empty space. All beings are included in this true and actual Dharma, irrespective of whether it's the Buddha, or a heavenly demon, or one of outside ways--none can get out of the Dharma Realm. So the heavenly demons and those of outside ways eventually have to comply with the Proper Dharma. Why? Because they can't destroy it. The Proper Dharma is indestructible. Nobody can destroy the true Dharma. If it can be destroyed, then it's not the true and actual Dharma. Because the true and actual Dharma can't be ruined.

THIS COMFORTABLE, GREAT BRIGHT LIGHT UNIVERSALLY APPEARS IN THE WORLD. This refers to the perfect cultivation of the Zero, which then manifests as the great storehouse of brilliant light. The storehouse of great bright light exhausts empty space and the Dharma Realm. It universally shines throughout the world in order to instruct all living beings to end birth and be free of death. It is just the Dharma-door of returning the light and reversing the illumination; returning to the root and going back to the source. This is your great wisdom light which destroys all your ignorance so your original Dharma nature can shine. Even if you don't believe this, go ahead and try it out, and then when the time comes, when it happens to you, there will be no way that you won't believe it. If you don't believe it, you'll still have to believe it, because that's the way it is, and what method would you have for not believing?

The great, brilliant storehouse is your own. It's not something other people give to you. It's not something that the Buddhas can give you. It's your own; it's inherent within yourself.

* * * * *

DIFFUSE THE ATOM BOMB IN YOUR MIND... GET OUT OF THE TURNING WHEEL

All the disasters in the world happen because people don't hold the Five Precepts and practice the Ten Good Acts. If everyone could hold the Five Precepts and follow the Ten Good Deeds, then all the disasters in the world would disappear. Just consider people's killing karma. The spirit of killing has really reached to the heavens. It is not just the killing karma of one person which has reached the heavens, but the killing karma of everyone has soared to the heavens. It's as if everyone harbors an atom bomb which is about to blow up. What's meant by the "atom bomb" that each person has? It's that person's afflictions. The momentum that has gathered from the afflictions of everyone is greater than the energy of an atom bomb. Just take a look. All the people throughout the world now have big tempers, they have lost their decency, and they've all turned into asuras. Asuras are solid in fighting. From morning to night they don't think of anything else but how to wage war against people--how to set off some type of weapon in order to destroy the opposition. It's the case that almost everyone in the world now has this type of thinking. They all want to destroy the other guy. And because of this, a killing-energy pervades the three thousand great thousand worlds. This evil, vile energy fills up the atmosphere and causes many people to get weird sicknesses. Once they contract these types of diseases, they can't get well. No matter how progressive science is, there's no way to come up with a cure for these illnesses. Why is that? It's because the karma of killing has grown too heavy. Because the karma of killing is so heavy, it contributes to both man-made disasters and natural calamities. Earthquakes and other kinds of violent phenomena appear. Weird and incurable diseases abound. Once one contracts them, one cannot be saved. The karma of killing is the basis of all this upheaval and turmoil.

Again, notice how many people are blind, deaf, or mute. People who can't hear or talk are those who have created too much killing-karma. This killing-karma does not begin and end with this present life, but extends back to all the evil karma that has been created since beginningless kalpas. When such people created killing karma, they fell into the hells. Then they turned into hungry ghosts, and eventually they became animals. After being animals for awhile, bit-by-bit they recovered their higher capacities and finer intelligence and became humans again. But even after being reborn as humans, their six faculties are not complete. Perhaps they are completely without eyes or ears. Or they may have the sense organs themselves but not their functions. Perhaps their noses are defective, or their tongues do not work properly. In general, the six organs of eyes, ears, nose, tongue, body and mind are not perfect and complete. They must undergo that kind of retribution. Mutes don't know how to speak, all because of excessive killing-karma created in the past. Various different kinds of causes and conditions combine and lead to the retribution of being mute in this life.

One of the major reasons is that in the past they did not get to meet the Orthodox Buddhadharma, nor did they get to study under a Good and Wise Teacher. Without such opportunities, they fell further and further down. Once one falls into the six paths of rebirth, it's very hard to get out. The six paths are: gods, humans, asuras--the three good paths; and hell beings, hungry ghosts, and animals--the three evil destinies. When one does good and creates merit and virtue, then one is born into the good paths. But when one makes offenses and bad karma and transgresses, one is born into the three evil paths. The ancients put it very well in verse:

>   Out of the horse's belly, and into a donkey's womb,
>   How many times have you gone back and forth
>   before King Yama's Hall?
>   You've just passed by Lord Shakra's Palace,
>   Only to end up being fried in the pot of King Yama.

People in this world are not born as people every time. Sometimes they are born as horses or donkeys or cows. They continue to "hang out" at King Yama's Hall, like a guest who seems unwilling to leave. It isn't known how many times you have passed by his place. On the other hand, Lord Shakra's Palace is really luminescent and you have occasionally been by this royal palace, too. How did you happen to pass by Lord Shakra's Palace? It's because you were on your way to being born in the heavens. However, eventually you always end up in the frying pot of King Yama again. There, King Yama fries you in oil fat. And so it goes, as you revolve around the six paths.

It's really dangerous! There is no guarantee that in every life you will be able to practice good and create merit and virtue. There will certainly be times when you create offenses, transgressions, and evil karma. So sometimes you are born high, and sometimes you fall. Even as people, we are very muddled, we can't discriminate things very clearly. Nor can we tell exactly which direction we are headed in.

There are many different heavens included in the path of gods. The Heaven of the Four Kings, the Trayastrimsha Heaven, the Suyama Heaven, the Heaven of Peace and Comfort, and the Heaven of the Comfort from Others' Transformations. There are many different levels of heavens, and the living beings in each of them enjoy different kinds of blessings and rewards. But even the worse kind of suffering in the heavens is better by far than the best type of enjoyment found in this realm. Therefore, when people rise to the heavens, they don't want to come back down.

Then there's the path of the asuras. They are born in the heavens and have heavenly blessings, but not heavenly virtue, and therefore they don't have heavenly authority. They don't have the virtuous conduct of heavenly beings, so they don't have any power. And their name also means "no wine." That means that in the heavens they don't get any wine to drink. Because of that they want to fight for some wine. They are always battling with Lord Shakra. They want to usurp his position as King. So you could say that asuras are just the brigands of the heavens. We have bandits in the human realm and the heavens have their bandits, too.

Asuras revolt against Lord Shakra, the Jade Emperor, who is just Lord God. They are always waging war against the heavenly troops and heavenly generals and often they defeat the Jade Emperor. Wars do happen even in the heavens. You shouldn't think it's all peaceful up there. After being born in the heavens, and completely using up their blessings, the beings there still have to fall. Then they might become cows or horses--it's not known for sure. Therefore, revolving within the six paths is absolutely too dangerous! You shouldn't linger on for the rewards of the heavens or the enjoyments of the human realm. The rewards of the heavens are not reliable, and even less so are the rewards of the human realm. So don't wait until you fall into the three evil destinies to think about cultivating, because then you won't get the chance. It's easier to cultivate in the human realm to become a Buddha. But once outside of the human realm, it's not easy at all.

*****

FIRST, CURE THE CANCER OF YOUR OWN MIND

The world today is filled with terror. People of all races are in a perpetual state of fear, so that they don't feel safe when they walk about, they can't taste the food they eat, and they can't sleep peacefully. What's the principle behind this? Why has such a state appeared? Those who believe in Buddhism should pay particular attention to the principle governing this phenomenon. It's because the evil offenses and evil karma that people are creating are filling up the heavens. Each person keeps creating more karma and never makes an attempt to eradicate the karma that gets amassed. Everyone has committed the karma of killing, stealing, sexual misconduct, taking intoxicants, and lying. It is simply because people do not maintain and uphold precepts which govern these five actions that slowly, bit by bit, the karma accumulates. When the karma from killing living beings becomes great enough, the energy of animosity will completely fill up the three thousand great thousand world systems.

Every kind of living being that is killed carries with it a kind of vengeful poisonous energy. For instance, if a pig is killed, it generates a vengeful energy. And when a cow is killed, its mind brings forth its own particular brand of resentment and hatred that is very lethal. It is that kind of poison which is now filling up the three thousand great thousand worlds. Whatever kind of living being is killed emits its own kind of vengeful energy, making not just one single kind of vengeful energy, but many kinds. When all those different kinds of vengeful energies meet and combine they cause people to get really weird sicknesses. Cancer is one example of this. No matter what kind of medicine one uses, cancer cannot be cured. Why? It's because the poison which brings it about is so fierce. When you try to use any single kind of medicine to cure an illness caused by such a fierce poison, it will not be effective. Cancer comes about from a combination of many different kinds of poisons, and no matter what single method one uses to try to cure it, it cannot be cured.

There is only one way that cancer can be cured. One must change one's heart around. Change your direction. Change all the mistakes you made in the past. Only then can your sickness be cured. If you refuse to change, then of course the sickness cannot leave. So in the world today, there appear all kinds of strange illnesses which go beyond the imagination, and they all come from the energy of vengeance. If it gets worse, we will experience such disasters as atomic bombs and plutonium plant accidents, or strong winds, floods and earthquakes, or the sky falling-- all such kinds of problems and disasters will occur, which will make this world even more fearful to live in.

Such a world as this is caused from the karma of living beings. If you want the world to change, the first thing you must do is clean out all the poison from your own heart. When there is no more poison of greed, hatred and stupidity in your mind, then the poison in your world will also be eradicated. But if it's the case that the greed, hatred, and stupidity in your mind keeps on increasing, getting fiercer and fiercer each day, then of course the disasters in the world will just become worse and worse as the days go by.

The Buddha said, "Everything is created from the mind alone." What is being discussed here gives evidence to that principle. Everything in the world that occurs comes from the minds of people. All the things that are happening right now are happening because of the minds of people. If people of the world want disasters to be eradicated, they must first begin within their own minds. That is to say, they must be sure that in their own minds there is 1) no greed, 2) no fighting, 3) no seeking, 4) no selfishness, and 5) no interest in self benefit.

Each person who can do that will be able to eliminate the vengeful energy from his own world. The same principle applies, whether referring to two, three, four, five, a thousand, or ten thousand people. If that many people apply these principles to their daily lives, then their worlds will be peaceful. If everyone can practice those Five Conditions, then even if we weren't seeking peace, peace would naturally and spontaneously occur. All disasters and unlucky events would disappear. Each of us has the responsibility to make this world a better place, that is, to change our own minds and hearts, to change from evil and go towards the good. This is the most profound and ultimate way of preventing disasters from happening. All those of you who have heard this principle today should actually put into practice: no greed, no fighting, no seeking, no selfishness, or no interest in self benefit. That's the way to prevent war.

In the Dharma-ending Age, very few people believe in the Proper Dharma any more. But the teachings of outside-way sects are believed wherever they appear. That's another reason why the world is getting worse. Moreover, there's a kind of scholar who investigates the Buddhadharma as if it were just another worldly dharma, and never uses the Buddhadharma to cultivate. Those who fall into this category just do research on Buddhism's principles. When they investigate in that way, they are unable to tell the difference between what's true and what's false, what's right and what's wrong. Therefore they take the false to be true and what's authentic to be phoney. That kind of evil knowing teacher without any eyes, who claims to understand without ever having understood, who appears to know something but actually knows nothing, that kind of scholar takes the Sutras, Vinaya, and Shastras of Buddhism and criticizes them all. Such "scholars" say, "This Sutra is questionable and we should investigate it. It should be thoroughly researched." But before they finish their research they die, and yet even though they have died, they have harmed those people who remain in the world. That is because if there are people with faith in the Buddhadharma who encounter the results of such research, it causes them to have doubts, to the point that although they once believed, many will then retreat from the Buddhadharma and lose their proper faith. One could say that such scholars are the sons and grandsons of demon kings who have come into the world for the purpose of destroying the Buddhadharma. They destroy the Buddhadharma in order to cause people to fall and lose their vision, their eyes. They cause living beings to walk down a dark road, a very dangerous road. At present there are books, magazines, and other literature which claim that *The Teaching From the Mind of the Third Patriarch* is phoney, that actually a man by the name of Lun Huan wrote it and that the Third Patriarch claimed it as his own work. They claim that they have discovered the "inside scoop." They also say that the *Song of Enlightenment* of Master Yung Chia was put together by a number of different people. I refuse to believe that the Patriarchs of the past were without any self-respect and took others' work, claiming it to be their own. I don't believe that they would steal others' gold and put it on their own face. So those with wisdom shouldn't believe in such deviant knowledge and views. They shouldn't be confused about true principle. This is very important.

* * * * *

WHITE UNIVERSE
by, Venerable Master Hua

Ice in the sky
Snow on the ground,
Tiny creatures beyond number die in the cold,
Or sleep in hibernation.
Contemplate in the midst of stillness;
Investigate in the midst of movement.
Dragons wrestle and tigers fight in constant sport,
Ghosts cry and spirits wail, in strange magical
  transformations.
The meaning of what is truly real
Is severed from words;
It cannot be thought of.
You should go forward quickly.

With the great and the small destroyed,
With no inside and no outside,
Every mote of dust
Contains the entire Dharmarealm.
Complete, whole, and perfectly fused,
Interpenetrating without obstruction.
With two clenched fists, shatter the cover of empty
  space,

> *Swallow in one mouthful the source of the ocean of*
> *Buddhalands.*
> *With kindness and compassion rescue everyone.*
> *Spare neither blood nor sweat,*
> *And never pause to rest.*

COMMENTARY:

    I wrote this poem in 1972. In Chinese, this poem is an exact match for the famous poem written by the Chinese hero Yao-fei, of the Sung Dynasty. Yao-fei was a big general, and he killed many, many people--to the point that the entire Yang Tze River was dyed red with their blood. The poem he wrote was called, "Red River," and I have matched it word for word with, "White Universe." When I wrote this poem at Gold Mountain Monastery in 1972, not only did a river turn white, but the entire universe turned white. Why is it "white?" As you know, Gold Mountain Monastery is called, "the icebox." It's very, very cold there. In fact, it's gotten so cold that everything has turned white! That's talking about the "universe," on a small scale. Then, if you want to talk about it in a bigger scale, "universe," in Chinese is composed of two characters, (宇-yü 宙-chou); one referring to the zenith and nadir, the other to the four cardinal directions. So, the "universe" encompasses the six directions. Everything within it has turned white. There's not the least bit of darkness in it.

    How did this poem come to be titled, "White Universe"? In 1972, at Gold Mountain Monastery, we had a recitation session which lasted for seven days. During this time, participants recited, "OM MA NI PAD MI HUM"--the mantra of the Six Magic Syllables. This session was special in another way as well. It was held day and night, non-stop. "Day and night," isn't just a figure of speech here. The session was conducted 24 hours a day, literally. People worked in shifts, and took turns resting so that the mantra continued in the Buddhahall non-stop. The reason for doing this session was to seek world peace, and to get rid of all disasters. During that period of time, there were always rumors that San Francisco was going to fall into the ocean because of an earthquake. We had to recite this mantra to settle the earth so it wouldn't quake. So, we decided to maintain the recitation of the mantra day and night, and not slack off--not skimp on materials. All through it we were fighting with the heavenly demons, and those of outside ways; they wanted the earth to quake, but I didn't want the earth to quake. So, we just turned things around, and nobody was allowed to be lazy. Everybody who participated in the session was very, very vigorous. I didn't participate; I was behind the scene acting as supervisor. I have radar, you know, so I would have known if anyone had slept when they were supposed to be reciting. I checked out my radar during those seven days, and nobody ever fell asleep when they were reciting. They were really working very hard; that made me very happy, because what makes me most happy is to see people cultivating. What makes me most unhappy is when people do things to cheat others. For example, if any of my disciples who have left the home life still go around doing very false things, I find that intolerable.

After those seven days had passed, I wrote this poem in commemoration of that occasion. I don't care whether the poem is good or not. Basically, I don't even know what's good and what's bad;I don't make those discriminations. However, I will recite it here for you now, and explain it.

ICE IN THE SKY/ SNOW ON THE GROUND/ Why "ice"? Because Gold Mountain is the "icebox." "Ice" also means it's totally hopeless. There's no hope, because there's no life. So, when you come here, don't even have expectations about being treated warmly. People at Gold Mountain Monastery are really cold, and don't have any warmth at all! *TINY CREATURES BEYOND NUMBER DIE IN THE COLD,/* These "creatures" are all the microorganisms in our bodies, all the bacteria and all the germs. These are the worms that have died. So, you can say there were no "worms," because the worms were all dead. There was no warmth, and there were no worms. Why did these creatures die? Because they all need vitamins. People need vitamins A, B, C, D,and all the others to survive. However, at Gold Mountain, it was so cold that the worms couldn't make it. They either died or went to *SLEEP IN HIBERNATION/* When that happens another scene arises. So, the poem goes on to say: *CONTEMPLATE IN THE MIDST OF STILLNESS;/* When it's cold everything becomes very still, very quiet. What are quieted are your seven passions, and your six desires. They have been quelled, and you are really quiet as you singlemindedly recite, OM MA NI PAD MI HUM, without stop. When you recite like this in stillness, you also *INVESTIGATE IN THE MIDST OF MOVEMENT./* From within the stillness arises a certain movement. Some very strange things happen. What do you start to see? *DRAGONS WRESTLE AND TIGERS FIGHT IN CONSTANT SPORT,/* You suddenly see dragons riding the clouds and driving the fog, as well as tigers leaping over gorges and mountains.

They are playing about in sport. It's something very exciting to behold; sort of like watching a kaleidoscope. It is very entertaining. That's one state that arises. Also, *GHOSTS CRY AND SPIRITS WAIL, IN STRANGE MAGICAL TRANSFORMATIONS./* Something happens when you are contemplating in stillness, when you are meditating. States appear. You see ghosts and spirits, and they are wailing and weeping, but it's all an illusory state. The ghosts cry, "Oh, please come and save me! My karmic obstructions are so heavy!" The spirits counter them and say, "No, no, don't bother with them, they are just karmic ghosts!" So there they are having it out with one another. While this is all going on, we know that it is just an illusory state, a transformed state; it's not true. So, you ask, "What is true?" *THE MEANING OF WHAT IS TRULY REAL/ IS SEVERED FROM WORDS;/* The true and actual meaning is beyond words. What is true? What is true cannot be said. It cannot be expressed. It cannot be described through duality, because true meaning is not long, not short; not good, not bad; not correct, not incorrect; not right, and not wrong. *IT CANNOT BE THOUGHT OF/* It's inconceivable and ineffable! However, at this point, does it mean that we don't go ahead to pursue this thing since it's so hard to reach and so unfathomable? No. The poem says, *YOU SHOULD GO FORWARD QUICKLY./* Even when it's so difficult, even when it looks like it is not tangible at all, you still have to be very, very vigorous and push ahead; pursue this true meaning.

   This is the only poem of its type that I've written. It's the first one I ever wrote and it will probably be the last. The reason is because I don't like to get caught up in words. If you get hung-up in words, then you face the obstruction of language; if you get attached to the mark of language, that's not a very good thing.

   The poem continues to explain this state *WITH THE GREAT AND THE SMALL DESTROYED,/ WITH NO INSIDE AND NO OUTSIDE,/* Greatness as vast as the universe, and smallness as minute as a dust-mote all vanish. All such discriminations are gone. It's not inside, it's not outside, and it's not in the middle. However, *EVERY MOTE OF DUST,/ CONTAINS THE ENTIRE DHARMAREALM./* This true meaning can be found within every single particle of dust. Every minute mote contains the true and actual meaning, and pervades the entire Dharmarealm. *COMPLETE, WHOLE, AND PERFECTLY FUSED,/* The true meaning is limitless, and yet it is also one. It's one and it's many; it's many and it's one. The one doesn't obstruct the many; the many doesn't obstruct the one. One and many are mutually non-obstructive; they are one completely fused body. It's like lights shining upon one

another. When many lights shine upon one another, one light doesn't fight with the other lights and say, "You're blocking out my light. I can't shine brightly, because $you're$ here!" Lights don't contend in that way. They are mutually interpenetrating and increase each other's brightness. That's the kind of state that is talked about here, one which is *INTERPENETRATING WITHOUT OBSTRUCTION.*/
WITH TWO CLENCHED FISTS, SHATTER THE COVER OF EMPTY SPACE,/ With two fists clenched together, I am going to break apart even the cover of the entire void. Now you ask, "Does empty space actually have a lid?" No, but we still must break through it. I'm willing to shatter the entire void to smithereens! What does this mean? It means that, "originally, there wasn't even a single thing. So how could dust alight?" Not only that, but I can *SWALLOW IN ONE MOUTHFUL THE SOURCE OF THE OCEAN OF BUDDHALANDS.*/ There are innumerable Buddha countries--this world, that world, and limitless other worlds, uncountable universes, one upon another. But I can take all of these worlds in and swallow them in one mouthful. Someone is wondering, "How strange to be able to swallow that many worlds. Are you a freak or something?" Well, if I am a freak and if I have powers like that, it's okay. It's not bad being a "freak." When this state occurs, you are totally unobstructed. There is no restraint and no hang-ups. You are absolutely free!
   What happens then? *WITH KINDNESS AND COMPASSION RESCUE EVERYONE.*/ It's not that you attain this state and say, "I have it made, and I'm not going to do anything any more." Rather, you exhaust all your efforts; you bring forth great kindness and compassion to save all living beings, and as long as there is a single living being who has not been saved, you won't stop. You won't stop until all living beings are saved. So the poem ends, *SPARE NEITHER BLOOD NOR SWEAT,*/ *AND NEVER PAUSE TO REST.*/ This means one is not afraid of difficulties, one is not afraid of suffering; one is not afraid of having no money. You just go forward without stop, and be just as vigorous as it is possible for you to be.

   A. The poem, *WHITE UNIVERSE* was written by Venerable Master Hua, in the Spring of 1972, at Gold Mountain Monastery in San Francisco; it was translated by Bhikshu Heng Kuan.
   B. The Commentary was translated by Bhikshuni Heng Tao; Edited by Bhikshuni Heng Hsien, Gold Wheel Temple, 1982

THE THREE CORPSE SPIRITS AND NINE WORMS

All the dharmas within the universe are relative dharmas. This means they are complimentary to each other--they go in pairs. Therefore, good compliments evil, right compliments wrong, yin compliments yang, brightness compliments darkness, demons compliment Buddhas, and so forth. In Way-places where there are true cultivators, then it's for certain that demons are also not far behind. Demons come to help cultivators, to urge them on. And cultivators can influence demons to become good. Therefore, they mutually aid each other. So although on the outside, demonic obstacles seem to be undesirable, in actuality, cultivators should not pit themselves against demons. As it is said:

> *If there is no evil, then the good can't be revealed.*
> *If there are no unfilial children, then the filial ones won't be made apparent.*
> *If there is no treachery, then loyalty won't come forth.*
> *If there is no failure, then success won't follow.*

It works the same way with demons. If a Way Place is very mediocre, very common, then demonic obstacles won't arise. But in a large Way Place where people are truly trying to cultivate, then demonic obstacles will certainly appear. Even then, we should try to look at the positive and brighter side of the picture. As I tell you often:

> *Demons come to polish the Way,*
> *Those on the true way have to endure demons.*
> *The more you get polished, the brighter you get;*
> *You'll be polished until you're like the autumn moon,*
> *Which illumines all the demon hordes in empty space.*
> *When the demon hordes are scattered,*
> *Then the original Buddha manifests.*

As for true cultivators, "inside there is no body and mind, and outside there is no world." They are not greedy for wealth, sex, fame, food or sleep. They've cut off the five roots of the hells. On the other hand, false cultivators are very fond of the five desires. So right there is another example of complimentary dharmas. By the same principle, people who have Way virtue wish to ascend, while people lacking virtue will fall. There are some who can see through everything and put it all down, and there are those who cannot see through anything nor can they put anything down.

But when you come down to it, putting everything down and seeing through it all really isn't so easy. People who are readily able to put everything down, who are in a state of "thus, thus unmovingness, constantly bright and clear", who aren't turned by the eight winds, are people who have cultivated for hundreds of thousands of millions of asamkhyeya kalpas--it's not known for how long. As for those who can't see through things or put things down, they are people who have just started to cultivate. They haven't even entered the door! Such people find it very hard to put down their attachment to people and dharmas. Everywhere they encounter thorns and thickets, and they always feel that others are rotten to them. Even if they clearly are in the wrong, they still rationalize for themselves and do not admit their mistakes. People like that are hard to save. They are like people suffering from a terminal illness and who still remain completely without shame and remorse. They act as their own defense attorneys. When this matter is investigated at its source, it is found to be the Three Poisons acting up again.

Lao Tze said, "If one is able to constantly chase out one's desires, then one's mind will naturally be still. If one can clarify one's heart, then one's spirit will naturally be pure. Quite spontaneously, then, the six desires will not even arise and the three poisons will be eradicated."

"If one is able to constantly chase out one's desires, then one's mind will be naturally still." "Constantly" means always and forever. One is at it all the time, without ever letting up or growing lax. "To be able" means to make a firm resolve to do it, to bring forth true determination, firmness, and great wisdom. To "chase out" means to drive away, to cast out. "Desires" include desire for all things--for food, sex, fame, sleep, and so forth. It is desires that cloud our minds and make us stupid. If you can constantly chase out your desires, then your mind will naturally be still.

"If one can clarify one's heart, then one's spirit will naturally be pure." This is also what Great Master Shen Hsiu meant when he said in his gatha:

> *The body is a Bodhi tree,*
> *The mind a bright mirror stand.*
> *Time and time again brush it clean;*
> *Do not let dust alight.*

Our minds are as if polluted with sediment and grit, therefore at all times we have to clean them out. What is sediment and sand? It's just false thoughts. False thoughts have muddled the water of our self-nature. If we purify this water, then our spirit will naturally become pure again.

In this way, "quite spontaneously, the six desires will no longer arise, and the three poisons will be eradicated." The six desires refer to the desire for the six sense objects-- sights, sounds, smells, tastes, objects of touch, and dharmas. The three poisons refer to greed, anger and stupidity. That's the way we talk about them in Buddhism. In Taoism, they are called the Three Corpse Spirits. And today I will give you a brief introduction to them.

The Three Corpse Spirits dwell within our bodies, acting as spies who report on us on whatever good or bad deed we have done. On the days of k'eng shen and chia tzu (according to Chung Kuo stems and branches calendar system), they go up to the heavens to make their report. The three corpse spirits are:

1) The Upper Corpse, called P'eng Chu, who lives on the upper third of the human body (also known as the Upper-Warmer). On the mornings of k'eng shen and chia tzu, this upper corpse spirit ascends to the heavens and reports on every single act you've carried out with the upper region of your body.
2) The Middle Corpse, called P'eng Chih, dwells in the middle section of the body (known as the Middle-Warmer). At noontime of k'eng shen and chia tzu days, this spirit ascends to the heavens and reports on all the deeds whether good or bad, you've carried out with the middle region of your body.
3) The Lower Corpse, called P'eng Sh'iao, lives in the lower section of the body (also known as the Lower-Warmer). On the nights of k'eng shen and chia tzu days, this spirit goes up to heaven and makes a complete report of everything you do with the lower region of your body.

They tell absolutely everything, hiding nothing. Now in Buddhism, the Three Corpse Spirits are called Greed, Anger, and Stupidity. Greed abides in the Upper Warmer, Anger abides in the Middle Warmer, and Stupidity abides in the Lower Warmer. These Three Corpse Spirits can also be called Corpse Ghosts.

The Upper Corpse has a specific location. It lodges in the bone which slightly protrudes from the back of the cranium, the occipital protuberis, and it is called the Yu Chen Kuan. This spirit lodges at that gate, guarding it, and monitoring a person's brainwaves. This is the first of the three big "gates" that a cultivator has to break through in order to have any success in his cultivation.

The Middle Corpse Spirit lodges in the middle of the spinal column, the Chia Chi Kuan. That's the second gate.

The Lower Corpse Spirit lodges at the Wei Lu Kuan--the coccyx--the very tip of the spinal column. That's where this spirit lives.

Those are the Three Gates, very hard to break through. Not only are there Three Gates, there are also Nine Worms, the nine "ku," which dwell in different parts of our bodies. Why do people sometimes catch "ku" poison, that is, get hexed? It's because within our own bodies we have these ku worms, and so if we're not careful we can catch a poison from the outside which conjoins with the worms inside.

What are these Nine Worms called? The first, "Big Brother," is called Crouching Worm (Fu Ku); the second is called Dragon Worm (Lung Ku); the third, White Worm (Pai Ku); the fourth, Flesh Worm (Jou Ku); the fifth, Red Worm (Ch'ih Ku); the sixth, Splitting Worm (Ke Ku); the seventh, Lung Worm (Fei Ku); the eighth, Stomach Worm (Wei Ku); and, the ninth, Intestinal Worm (Ch'ang Ku). Each of them lodges in a different part of the body, guarding the nine crevices.

Whereas the three "gates" mentioned earlier are large openings, these nine crevices are smaller cracks, like little holes. It's not at all easy to get through them, for the nine worms are constantly creating mischief and making it difficult for the cultivator to come to any success. Let's list their functions and locations.
1. The first worm, Crouching Worm, is so named because it crouches. Curled up like a ball, it is seemingly dormant. It sleeps by the occipital protuberis, the Yu Chen Ch'iao.
2. The second worm is Dragon Worm, because it is shaped like a little dragon. It hides in the nape of the neck, the ligament that joins the head with the shoulder blades, at the T'ien Ch'u Ch'iao.
3. The third worm is White Worm, which abides in the T'ao Tao Ch'iao, a section of the digestive tract where the solids separate from the liquids. This variety of worm is just the fatty tissues and lymph nodes in our body which are whitish in color.
4. The fourth, is the Flesh Worm, because it looks like a blob of flesh. It lives in the Shen Tao Ch'iao, the "pathway of the heart," and monitors our spirit. This is the worm which is responsible for heart trouble.
5. The fifth is the Red Worm, because it is a scarlet color. It dwells in the Ch'ia Chi Ch'iao, the spinal column.
6. The sixth is the Splitting Worm, which lives in the Hsüen Shu Ch'iao, the "gateway of mystery." It also rules over a part of the digestive system.

7. The seventh is the Lung Worm, which lives in the <u>Ming Men Ch'iao</u>, the Life-Gate crevice and rules over the lungs.
8. The eighth is the Stomach Worm, which lives in the <u>Lung Hu Ch'iao</u>, the Tiger and Dragon crevice, which is the seat of the reproductive organs.
9. The ninth is the Intestinal Worm, which lives in the <u>Wei Lu Ch'iao</u>, at the tip of the spinal column, and presides over the large intestine.

    Some of these worms are responsible for the maladies of the different organs. For example, the Lung Worm is responsible for lung diseases, the Stomach Worm is responsible for digestive problems, and the Intestinal Worm is responsible for intestinal disorders and so forth.

    Above has been a brief and general explanation of the Three Corpse Spirits and the Nine Worms. They are undercover agents who specialize in sabotaging a cultivator's efforts, making it difficult for him to go towards the good. They constantly urge you not to cultivate but to go out to play. Most of us aren't even aware that right within our own bodies there are these really undesirable elements. Moreover, the Three Corpse Spirits and Nine Worms have impressive powers. They can transform into gold, silver and valuable jewels, or beautiful forms in your dreams to come to entice you.

    They can either make you happy and seduce you, or make you terribly afflicted and depressed. Therefore, when you have certain dreams do not be overjoyed, thinking them to be magical responses. They could be very well be the Three Corpses and Nine Worms playing tricks on you. Don't be cheated by them.

DO THE REAL THING AND DO IT WELL

Within Buddhism there is the Dharma door of inquiring into Ch'an, the Dharma door of studying the teachings, the Dharma door of the Vinaya School, the Dharma door of the esoteric school, and there's the Pure Land Dharma door. The Dharma door of the Ch'an school is straightforward--it points directly at the mind. It is the Dharma door of seeing the nature and becoming a Buddha--that Dharma door. Within this door, not even a single dharma is set up--it is the Dharma door of returning to the origin. Now we are having this Ch'an ch'i (literally, Ch'an seven) to set aside a period of time so that people can obtain certification. A certain period of time is set up so that people can definitely become enlightened. Because of this, we don't do the regular morning and evening recitations and we don't even bow to the Buddhas, but instead work single-mindedly so as to inquire and awaken. Why don't we do morning and evening recitations or bow to the Buddhas? Because it is feared that the hard work you put into Ch'an will be dissipated and that you won't be able to continue applying your skill uninterrupted. And so all the other activities we normally perform in the Way place are temporarily put aside so we can within a single mind, inquire into Ch'an. If you work hard in this way and you still don't get awakened, then you have really wasted your time.

When I was young, I participated in a lot of Ch'an sessions and in every session I stayed in the hall meditating and never left it. In the day time I was in the meditation hall for the walking meditation periods and the sitting meditation periods. And in the evening when it was time to sleep, I was also in the Ch'an hall--from 12 midnight to 2:30 A.M. I sat up and slept on the mat. At that time I didn't dare be muddled, not even for a single second. Why? Because I was afraid that if I was muddled even for a single second, I would have wasted the time and perhaps allowed the moment for enlightenment to slip by. So at all times I was mindful of being right there and never let go of the two words, "birth and death" in front of my eyes. That's what's meant by "painfully being mindful of birth and death" and working hard at Ch'an. I was this way when I was young.

Now, here in America, although there are those who believe in the Buddha and who study the Buddhadharma, the places where people are genuinely working hard are few, very few; there virtually aren't any places where people are really doing this work. It's often the case that you hear people *say* they are doing it, but in actuality, nothing's going on--a case of putting out a sheep's head and selling dog-meat. What they say they are doing and what actually takes place doesn't mesh. Places like that are many, many. Many of you have traveled for tens of thousands of miles to get to America, so if you now don't truly put forth your effort to cultivate, it would really be a waste of your time and money. At the City we are serious about doing things right. The Eternally-Dwelling is making offerings to everyone so that they can work hard and cultivate. At other Wayplaces, if they want to have a Ch'an session or a Buddha Recitation Session, they go all around looking for donors to support it, asking people to give money. Here at the City of Ten Thousand Buddhas, the Dharma assemblies for working at cultivation are held every year--there are really quite a few of them in a single year--but it has never been the case that we from the City have gone out and asked people to contribute to these Dharma assemblies. Instead, we make all sorts of sacrifices so as to give people an opportunity to work hard and attain the Way. Despite the difficulties that are caused, the Eternally-Dwelling sets up these opportunities for everyone. The left home people of the Eternally-Dwelling endure suffering and are patient with the toil, and they cultivate really hard, eating only one meal a day, getting up very early and going to bed very late, working all the time. Some work in the office, some work in the high school, some work in the elementary school, some translate Sutras, some maintain the grounds, some build--everyone is working. Although we ourselves are all working we feel that it's still not enough, so every year we hold Dharma assemblies, during which it's appropriate for people from the outside to use effort too, and cultivate. So when the Buddha Recitation began I told all of you, the people who are working here at the City of Ten Thousand Buddhas should not have any thoughts at all and you don't want to do anything else--just single-mindedly apply your effort at cultivation and cultivate well. That's all I hope, just this one thing.

TO CULTIVATE, GET RID OF YOUR EMOTIONS

I want to start by asking you a question: We all believe in Buddhism--what is the Buddha?
Answer: The Buddha is everything, and everything is the Buddha.
Abbot: What is everything?
Answer: Everything is one.
Abbot: Then why call it "everything"?
Answer: At one time it was just one, but then it got to be everything, and now it's going back to being one.
Abbot: Who makes it?
Answer: I think empty space makes it.
Abbot: If it's "empty space," how can it make anything?
Answer: When things got mixed together, they started a cycle.
Abbot: But if there are things, then it's no longer "empty space."
Answer: Oh yeah. Empty space wouldn't be empty in that case. Well, I don't know.
Abbot: Although she doesn't know, she still dares to try to answer. If everything is the Buddha, then is this cup the Buddha?
Answer: Yes.
Abbot: Then why don't you bow to it?
Answer: I could bow to it.
Abbot: Even if you bowed to it, it's not for sure that other people would recognize it as such and bow to it.

* * *

Another answer: A Buddha is one who is greatly kind and compassionate. He is greatly wise, has ended birth and death, and is greatly enlightened.
Abbot: How did he become enlightened?
Answer: By ending birth and death.
Abbot: How did he end birth and death, and how did he become enlightened?
Answer: From cultivating wisdom.
Abbot: Not bad, from cultivating wisdom.
Buddha means "Enlightened": the Buddha is an "Enlightened One." Whoever is enlightened is Buddha. Therefore, when people say they don't believe in the Buddha, they are saying they don't believe in enlightenment. What is meant by enlightenment? Enlightenment is just understanding. It is true understanding--wisdom. How does one come to have wisdom? It is from cultivating bit by bit. It doesn't come all in one fell swoop. It's not immediate. It's not cultivating today and becoming a Buddha tomorrow. And it's not like taking drugs-- dropping some pill for an instant high and figuring you can remain in control and not get addicted.

It doesn't work that way. You have to take up giving, take up holding precepts, take up patience, take up vigor, take up dhyana-samadhi, and take up Prajna wisdom, and in that way, cultivate bit by bit. It's got to be on a regular basis. In every instant you must go forward in your cultivation. As you cultivate, you increase your good roots. If you don't cultivate, then your good roots decrease.

A little while ago someone said to me that they had been working hard but had made no progress. If you really work hard, that itself is progress. Working hard itself is progress, while not working is regressing. Regressing and progressing just depend upon whether you are doing any cultivation or not. When you are truly progressing you're not thinking,"I'm cultivating so I should experience some sort of state; I should either see something, or hear some kind of sound, or some kind of feeling--which would mean I was making progress." If you're thinking that then you've gotten the wrong idea. Progress just means constantly cultivating. Just that is progress. I told the person,"I don't understand much of anything. I don't understand science, and I've never delved into philosophy, but I do understand about eating. So let's talk about that. Why do we eat? Is it the case that we seek some kind of progress in eating? It isn't. We eat to live. We want to live so we eat. If we didn't eat, we'd die. However, at Gold Mountain Monastery, there are two who didn't eat for thirty-six days, two times, and they didn't die, and another who went without eating thirty-six days once and didn't die. There are also fifteen or sixteen who didn't eat for eighteen days and didn't die. Nonetheless, that was special. You can't say all people can go without eating.

The same principle applies to cultivating. It is as matter of fact as eating. To do well at cultivation, you have to do it bit by bit. Don't seek progress, and don't seek to become enlightened. Don't seek to become a Buddha-- don't seek anything at all.

We eat in order to live, so we should ask ourselves-- what do we live for? It certainly shouldn't be that we live for the sake of eating! For what, then?

> To do meritorious deeds for the world.
> To do virtuous deeds for the people.
> To benefit all in the universe.

If I can help people, then I help people. If I can't help them, if my strength is insufficient, then I shouldn't force it. That's what we should live for--to help others. There are also those who say, "I live in order to become a Buddha." That's also okay. But you shouldn't seek to become a Buddha. Just go forward on the proper road, then you are certain to become a Buddha. You don't need to do any seeking. Seeking is still false thinking. You should cultivate the path of effortlessness and not seek anything.

> When you reach the point that you seek nothing,
> Then you have no worries.

Why do people have afflictions? It's just because they have something which they seek. It's very simple. People who gamble seek to win money . They take a bus or a plane to Las Vegas, or Reno, to play the slot machines, the one armed bandits--hoping to win the jackpot. Seeking to win money , they keep putting their money in, and the beast keeps eating it. They put in some more, and get robbed by the bandit. They came in with $100,000 and $99,000 gets eaten. Then they become afflicted: "If I'd known that was going to happen, I never would have come here to gamble. I'll never see my $100,000 again!" Well who told you to go gambling anyway? Who told you to gamble? You told yourself to gamble. Once you get afflicted it doesn't stop with you, yourself. You go home and beat your wife, yell at the kids--so someone else has to take the abuse. Why? Because you lost your money, and recklessly gave vent to your frustrations. It all started with seeking.

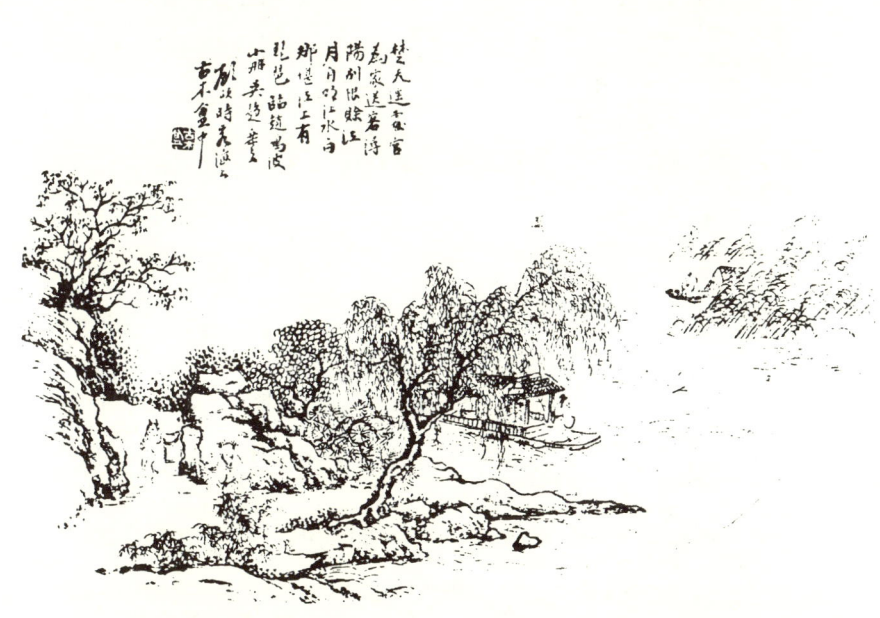

THE PRECEPT SASH

Now the weather has become quite cold, so people should wear more clothes. Although you may say that this body is false, we have to borrow this false body to cultivate what's true. So we should accord with the weather. In India, a country which has a hot climate, not only the left home people bare the right shoulder, but also many lay people do. That is because the climate is so warm. Also, with an exposed right shoulder, the right arm is freed to move around and do things. If the Buddha had been born in China, like for example the last seven Buddhas of Antiquity who were born in Hang Chou, then perhaps it would not have been necessary to uncover the right shoulder. But the *yi*, or precept sash, is something that lefthome people must wear, because the precept sash traditionally is worn so that lefthome people can manifest the appearance of a Bhikshu or Bhikshuni, and so they should wear the precept sash at all times.

In China there are people today who call themselves lefthome people but who never wear the precept sash. Why is that? We should investigate this matter very deeply. When Buddhism was first transmitted to Chung Kuo, the lefthome people wore the precept sash just as they do in the Theravada tradition today. At that time sashes were not worn with rings and hooks as they are nowadays. Lefthome people just wrapped a single piece of cloth around their bodies, leaving the right shoulder uncovered. When Buddhism was first transmitted to China, the lefthome people also wore the precept sash in this way, except that underneath the sash, they had to wear more clothing. Perhaps they wore cotton down or two layers of robes or some other kind of clothing in accord with the traditional dress of Chung Kuo. Why did they wear more clothing underneath their precept sashes? Because the weather was cold, not hot as in India. In such a cold climate if people didn't wear more clothes they wouldn't be able to take it. For that reason, lefthome people at that time wore lefthome clothes underneath the precept sash. And it was just because they wore clothes underneath their sashes that people would often lose their precept sash. Perhaps it would drop off while they were walking down the road single-mindedly reciting the Buddha's name, and later they wouldn't even be able to remember where it might have fallen off.

Left home people are very poor. As it's said,

The *poor Sanghan,* or

A *poor one of the Way.*

And since Sanghans are poor, they can't afford to replace any clothes that they might lose. Although Dharma protectors may make offerings to members of the Sangha, they only do so occasionally, and so if one loses one's precept sash, one couldn't have another one made to replace it, and so one would have to get along wearing only the long inner robe. For this reason, the lefthome people of Chung Kuo held a meeting and tried to devise a solution to losing the precept sash. Finally, there was a Patriarch who suggested that the precept sash be fastened with a ring and hook so that it couldn't fall off. After some further discussion, the assembly concluded that this was a practical solution, so from that time onward, the precept sash has been worn with a ring and hook. In this way people don't lose their precept sashes anymore. But still another problem arose with regard to wearing the precept sash. When people have to work they must remove the *yi* to prevent it from getting soiled and torn. After awhile, people began to feel that it was a waste of time to have to unfasten the hook and ring and remove the yi, and then put it back on and fasten the hook and ring each time. So people began to not bother to wear the precept sash at all during work times. There's a saying,

If a thing is done for a long time, it becomes a habit.

Because people got greedy to save time, they eventually just forgot the precept sash altogether. And this is how it came to be that people no longer wear the precept sash in Chung Kuo. It was just because of greed for convenience that those lefthome people flowed along with the lowly current. After such a habit went unchecked for a long time, people lost touch with the original tradition of wearing the precept sash to the point where they even forgot why lefthome people wore the precept sash in the first place. This is how the lefthome people of Chung Kuo evolved a new tradition of not wearing the precept sash. And then, when Buddhism was transmitted into Japan from Chung Kuo, not only did the lefthome people in Japan not wear the precept sash, but they didn't even bother to receive the precepts! So the further Buddhism spread out, the more the original traditions became totally washed out.

And so today, if one wears the precept sash, he is looked upon as a weirdo creature. People say of him, "This is not right. You're just trying to exhibit a special style!" Those who say such things have absolutely no understanding of what precepts and rules are all about. They are just like country bumpkins, and they don't have the faintest understanding of what Buddhism is about. They just assume that not wearing the precept sash is correct. Now that such a tradition has been set up, even some of the Theravaden monks don't wear the Samghati(big sash) anymore. And so now, wherever the Great Vehicle tradition in Buddhism is found, there is also found the tradition of not wearing the precept sash, and we owe this tradition to the people of Chung Kuo.

If people think that wearing the precept sash is wrong, then they should just forget it. Why then when they see people wearing the precept sash do they criticise them? Moreover, when those who don't ordinarily wear the precept sash attend the meal offering, they then don the precept sash. They also do this for the evening ceremony. What's the meaning behind this? People say, "Not wearing the precept sash is for the purpose of saving time." So why would they suddenly manifest the appearance of a Bhikshu for the ceremonies? How about the other times? Is it the case that lefthome people return to lay life at the times when they are not attending a ceremony? Is that why they do not display the appearance of a Bhikshu at those times? And why are they so opinionated about this subject? They take what's right as wrong and what's wrong as right. We should seriously look into the tradition of wearing the precept sash and find out the meaning behind it. There are those who call themselves disciples of the Buddha but who haven't the foggiest notion of the purpose behind wearing the precept sash--this is indeed a pitiful situation!

For reasons such as the ones mentioned above, this is called the Dharma Ending Age, the time when people don't understand or recognize the Dharma, so they don't know how to conduct themselves properly. And so bit by bit the Buddhadharma is disappearing.

We have now started Buddhism in the west. We shouldn't pay attention to the petty affairs of others. If people don't want to wear the precept sash it's their own business. Some people may say that we at the City of Ten Thousand Buddhas are trying to exhibit a special style. But that's okay. It doesn't matter what people slander us with. We just continue to go about doing what's right. They can criticize in whatever way they want to, but we should be very clear of our goal, of our aim. We should be clear about causes and retributions. We should know what's the original tradition and what is the origin of Buddhism. We should understand very clearly how all these traditions came about. We should be very clear why one should wear the precept sash--we should understand those principles very clearly. Just as all of us wear the precept sash today, so did I when I was in Chung Kuo. When I lived in Hong Kong I also wore the precept sash, and now in America, those who leave the home life under me also wear the precept sash. This is the tradition of Buddhism--it is the gesture of "manifesting the appearance of a Bhikshu." And so starting today, we will post a sign at the temple's Main Gate in two languages-- Chung Wen and English--saying that no matter what country Buddhists visiting the City of Ten Thousand Buddhas come from, during their stay here they should wear a precept sash. Of course, this refers only to lefthome people. We should establish this tradition of the Patriarchs of old.

    I realize that many people slander me now and say that the Buddhism which I transmit here is faulty. But I myself look into my own conscience and question myself in my every action. As much as I'm aware of what is the straight and proper thing to do, I go ahead and do it. Of course, if there's something that I'm not aware of, I don't do it. And so regarding the matter of the precept sash, all lefthome people should wear it at all times, in order to manifest the appearance of a lefthome person. Although one could say that we are just a small minority of people, but if we can continue to manifest the appearance of Bhikshus here, it means that the Orthodox Buddhadharma has not yet been cut off. Here we transmit the Proper Dharma and don't let it ever get cut off.

THE WAY HAS TO BE PRACTICED

What's spoken is Dharma,
What's practiced is the Way.
You can speak it wonderfully,
speak it well,
But if you don't actually practice,
it's not the Way.

Do you believe this principle or not? No matter how you can speak, it's not as good as being able to practice. If you can go ahead and practice, then you are a true and actual disciple of the Buddha. If you just talk but don't practice, then you're a false disciple of the Buddha. Therefore, all of us should return the light and reverse the illumination and ask ourselves, "Do we want to be true disciples of the Buddha, or do we want to be false disciples of the Buddha?" If you want to be a true one, then don't tell lies. Don't be selfish and don't be self-seeking.

The Way is traversed; it's practiced. So it also says,

Universal affection is humaneness,
Acting correctly is righteousness.
To go from here to there is the Way.
To be complete in oneself, and not rely
on externals, is virtue.

--*Essay on "The Original Source"*

"Universal affection is humaneness." I'll explain for you the meaning of affection. Universal means vast and expansive. Didn't Jesus talk about universal love? It means being good to everyone, even loving one's enemies. He was kind toward the people who wanted to do him in. He was cherishing and protective, compassionate and loving towards them. The "love" Jesus was talking about is certainly not the emotional love that men and women talk about. It was a kind of compassionate, kind, joyous, and benevicent love. There are those who misinterpret Jesus' intent, who've taken it to mean, "I *love* you, and you *love* me. I am in your bosom and you are in my heart." They've turned it into I-don't know what kind of drivel. What Jesus was talking about was that one should be kind and compassionate to people. No matter what kind of person they were, even murderers and arsonists, Jesus was good to them, saying, "I shall influence them to change their evil ways and become good; to mend their ways and start anew." That was Jesus' universal love. Universal affection is just humaneness. Humaneness means being human.

Yen Yüan inquired about humaneness. He asked Confucius, "What is meant by 'humaneness'?" The Master said, "Humaneness consists in submitting oneself to propriety." He said, "If you are able to curb your own desires, and submit them to natural principle, that is, the heavenly decree, then that is humaneness." That's why Han Yu says, "Universal affection is humaneness."

"Acting correctly is righteousness." When you do things and do them right, most appropriately, just as they should be done, then that is righteousness. Righteousness is knowing how and when to act. For example,

The great righteousness of Noble Kuang penetrates to heaven.

Kuang Ti Kung, has a very red face because of all the righteous energy that fills up his body. When he does things, he does them absolutely right. Even to the point that if he kills someone, it's only because he *should* kill that person. On the other hand, if he should save someone, then he would certainly save them. His righteousness is the same as heaven and earth, and so it is said to reach to heaven.

"To go from here to there is the Way." To go from one place to another place, that is the Way. How do we walk on the Way? By cultivating. In cultivating, going from one place to another is just the Way. You can say that going from a bad place to a good place is the Way. Turning great evil into great good, that is the Way.

"To be complete in oneself and not rely on externals is virtue." To be complete in oneself is to perfect one's own endowment with humaneness, righteousness, propriety, wisdom and trustworthiness. When one's humaneness, righteousness, propriety, wisdom and trustworthiness are perfect and complete, just that is virtuous conduct. How should you do it? By not killing, not stealing, not engaging in sexual misconduct, false speech and not taking intoxicants--holding the Five Precepts. By holding the Five Precepts, one attains to the Five Constants. The Five Constants are humaneness, righteousness, propriety, wisdom and trustworthiness.

In the same essay, Han Yu goes on to say,

Humaneness, righteousness, propriety, and wisdom

*are rooted in the mind.
They produce a color which naturally shows in one's
face, suffuses one's back, and lights up the
four limbs.
The four limbs speak without saying a word.*

    The qualities of humaneness, righteousness, propriety
and wisdom have their source in the mind. When you possess
them, they are evident on your face. Most people, when they
see you, feel good about you; they feel that you are worthy
of their respect and admiration. As for example, a greatly
virtuous high Sanghan--take Hsü Lao, for instance--certainly
would never have told people to be particularly good to him.
Their gaze would be riveted upon him and their eyes would
never want to leave him for an instant. Why is that? It's
because he was perfect in humaneness, righteousness, propriety, and wisdom, and he had virtuous conduct.
    "They produce a color which naturally shows in one's
face, suffuses one's back, and lights up the four limbs."
The glow flushes your face, and even can be discerned from
behind your back. All people have to do is see your back to
know, "This person is especially fine!" So when the bandits
saw the Venerable Hsü Lao, they all said, "Ah, Elder, Great
Gentleman, don't bother to move. Please remain seated. Please
don't be afraid." One time, some bandits held up the market-
place. They saw the Venerable Hsü Lao seated there and requested the Elder Master to remain seated in his place, saying, "We don't want anything from you." When they had stolen
everyone else's belongings, they bowed to the Venerable Master and went on their way. Why was that? Because he had
sufficient virtuous conduct. The bandits knew it and called
him "Elder Great Gentleman." At that time, the Venerable
Master had really long hair; hair at least two inches long,
and his beard was probably three inches long. The bandits
called him "Elder Great Gentleman," because he had merit
and virtue. Therefore, the essay says that this flow of
virtue,

          *Suffuses one's back, and
          lights up the four limbs.*

One doesn't have to say anything: everyone recognizes such
virtue. You don't have to say, "Do you recognize me? Do
you recognize me? I have great virtuous conduct. The merit
and virtue I have done is such that in heaven above and
earth below, there is no merit and virtue as great as mine."
One doesn't have to introduce oneself. All people have to

do is look to understand. That's the meaning of "humaneness, righteousness, propriety, and wisdom."
To continue Han Yu's essay, he goes on to say,

> *In fullness, there is beauty;*
> *In fullness and radiance there is greatness;*
> *Greatness transformed is sageliness;*
> *Sageliness that knows itself is spirituality.*

When the merit and virtue of humaneness, righteousness, propriety and wisdom are complete and full, then it's very beautiful, very fine. One doesn't need to use make-up and yet one is extremely adorned. "In fullness and radiance there is greatness." When humaneness, righteousness, propriety, and wisdom are complete and full, and a kind of radiant splendor appears, then one is known as a great person. Previously it said, a "beautiful"person. Now it is a "great" person.

"Greatness transformed is sageliness." In being great,one is also able to change and transform; if one has spiritual penetrations, then one is a Sage--a Sage who has certified to the fruit; perhaps an Arhat.

"Sageliness that knows itself is spirituality." If one is a Sage, say a fourth fruit Arhat, one still does not know completely. But if a Sage's knowledge encompasses and even transcends all the events within eighty thousand great kalpas, then his state enters the realm of "spirituality." He is one who is replete with spiritual powers, one who knows himself and everything else--a Bodhisattva. So, here we have the various levels of attainment of one who cultivates the transcendental Way: beauty, greatness, Sageliness, and spirituality.

Beautiful people, great people, Sagely people, and spiritual people. As for the spiritual:

> *One whom even the spiritual does not know is the Buddha.*

One whom the spiritual doesn't even know, is the Buddha. Therefore, when we cultivate, we should cultivate humanness, righteousness, propriety, and wisdom. Not killing is humaneness. Not stealing is righteousness. No sexual misconduct is propriety. Not engaging in false speech is sincerity. Not taking intoxicants is wisdom. If you don't kill, then you have a humane and loving attitude towards living beings.

If you don't steal, that is being in accord with righteousness. Not engaging in sexual misconduct is propriety. If all you do is practice sexual misconduct, then that is not in accord with propriety. Not to utter false speech is trustworthiness, and is the cultivation of sincerity and credibility. If you don't drink intoxicating beverages, then you are a person with wisdom. Not taking intoxicants includes not taking drugs--it includes not smoking marijuana, not taking LSD, not taking "happy pills" and so forth. Someone who can abstain from these things is someone with wisdom.

This day has gone by, and we have one day less. Do you believe that or not? If you try to get it back, you won't be able to. So we should not let the time go by in vain, and then, that's the very best.

* * * * *

QUESTION: Please explain the Three Sages of the West.

ABBOT: In the West, basically, there are a great many Buddhas and a great many Bodhisattvas, so why speak of just Three Sages? These Three Sages are Amitabha Buddha, along with Gwan Shih Yin Bodhisattva, and Great Strength Bodhisattva. In the past, before they reached Buddhahood, for life after life, they were Master and disciples. Amitabha Buddha was the Master, and Gwan Shih Yin Bodhisattva and Great Strength Bodhisattva were the disciples. Those three old cultivators made vows saying, "We want to establish a Land of Ultimate Bliss." What is meant by "Land of Ultimate Bliss"? In the Land of Ultimate Bliss one,

Endures none of the sufferings, but enjoys every bliss.

In that place there are no three evil destinies: no hell-beings, hungry ghosts, or animals. The three of them, the Master and his two disciples, made a trinity. The three made one substance--like Jesus, the Heavenly Lord, and the Holy Spirit, they were three in one. Now this is an analogy. It's not for sure it's just that way. They said they wanted to create a Land of Ultimate Bliss and in the future receive living beings who were undergoing suffering into the Land of Ultimate Bliss. Therefore, when Amitabha Buddha became a Buddha, Gwan Yin Bodhisattva made the vow to stand in for Amitabha Buddha and teach and transform living beings. Great Strength Bodhisattva also made the vow to stand in for his teacher and teach and transform living beings.

Therefore, they are called the Three Sages of the West. All people who recite the names of those three Sages can be reborn in the Land of Ultimate Bliss. However, this Dharma is spoken for people who want to rely on the "others" power. If you want to rely on your own power, then you cultivate Ch'an. If you want to have a dependent attitude and say, "Oh! Amitabha Buddha has vow-power; he is in the Western Land of Ultimate Bliss. If people recite his name then they are reborn in the Land of Ultimate Bliss!" That is to exclusively rely on Amitabha Buddha's power. If you are able to stand on your own, and want to become a Buddha in this very life, then you investigate Dhyana and sit in meditation-- it's just a different Dharma door. The Sixth Patriarch said, "People of the East want to be reborn in the West. So where should people of the West seek rebirth?" He was talking about kung fu (skill) of the mind ground. To use kung fu of the mind ground means that you don't develop a reliant attitude. You should learn to stand on your own. If you feel you can stand on your own, then investigate Ch'an. If you can't stand up, then cultivate Pure Land. If originally you can't stand up, but you recite the Buddha's name and reach the Pure Land, at that time you will be able to stand up. However, if you can stand up, but you don't cultivate, then you too can become someone who can't stand up. But we shouldn't just say, "Well, we don't want to rely on Amitabha Buddha, we want to cultivate ourselves." If you *cultivate*, then it counts. If you just give it lip service and say, "We want to cultivate," but don't cultivate, that's useless. So what I just said about "What's spoken is Dharma, what's practiced is the Way," is the same principle.

A SINGLE THOUGHT

> *If one wishes to know*
> *All the Buddhas of the three periods*
> *of time,*
> *One should contemplate the nature of*
> *the Dharma Realm;*
> *Everything is made from the mind alone.*

The Ten Dharma Realms are not apart from a single thought of the mind. This is the same principle.

If a person gives rise to a good thought, an auspicious spirit will come to protect them. If a person gives rise to an evil thought, a cruel spirit will trail them. The difference lies in a single thought. The ancients said,

> *If you take one single wrong step,*
> *You'll regret it for a thousand years.*

We can also say, "If you have a single wrong thought, you'll regret it for a thousand years." Good and evil are each contained in a single thought. I often say people's minds are like motes of dust, knocked around in space. Suddenly you're in the heavens, then suddenly among the animals, hungry ghosts, or in the hells.

There's no end to the bitter sea of suffering, so hurry up and come back to the other shore. There's nothing esoteric about it. It's simply a matter of getting rid of your bad habits and faults.

> No selfishness
> No seeking
> No greed
> No fighting
> No seeking for self-benefit

If you can follow these rules, you quite naturally won't go against heavenly principle or the hearts of people. If you can use these as a measure against your own actions each day, then you won't make any mistakes. Whether you want to be a person or to practice transcendental dharmas, you need these five principles as a guide.

If I say any more today, you'll just forget!

TRUE REPENTANCE AND REFORM

If each of us wants to change the dire situation of the world, we must change from the evil to the good; change our faults and renew ourselves. This will help the world return to a wholesome state of being. But if we don't change our faults and renew ourselves, then the world can only get worse and worse each day, and each day there will be an especially large number of calamities and disasters. So if we want to return this kalpa to a state of goodness, we should become replete with a heart of compassion. Everyone should at all times maintain a heart of great compassion and be filled with kindness, compassion, joy, and equanimity, thereby imitating the Four Unlimited Minds of the Buddha.

How can one be replete with kindness, compassion, joy, and giving? Kindness is the ability to bestow happiness. Compassion is the capacity to pull one out of suffering. With joy one is able to avoid worry, and equanimity increases one's virtue. If one wishes to have the abilities which result from those Four Unlimited Minds, first one should give rise to repentance within one's own mind. This repentance I speak of is true repentance, it's not just reciting the text of a repentance ceremony. Cultivators of the Way can contemplate *The Verse of Repentance of Universal Worthy Bodhisattva.*

UNIVERSAL WORTHY BODHISATTVA'S VERSE OF REPENTANCE AND REFORM

FROM BEGINNINGLESS TIME TO THIS PRESENT LIFE,
I HAVE SLANDERED AND DISRUPTED THE TRIPLE JEWEL,
ACTING AS AN ICCHANTIKA.
I HAVE DERIDED THE GREAT VEHICLE SUTRAS,
CUT OFF THE STUDY OF PRAJNA,
KILLED MY FATHER AND MOTHER,
AND SHED THE BUDDHAS' BLOOD.

I HAVE DEFILED THE SANGHARAMA,
BROKEN UP THE PURE CONDUCT OF OTHERS,
BURNED AND DAMAGED STUPAS AND TEMPLES,
AND STOLEN THE SANGHA'S PROPERTY.
THUS, GIVING RISE TO DEVIANT VIEWS,
I HAVE DENIED CAUSE AND EFFECT

I HAVE BEEN INTIMATE WITH EVIL COMPANIONS,
AND OPPOSED GOOD TEACHERS.
NOT ONLY HAVE I ENGAGED IN THESE DEEDS MYSELF,
I ALSO HAVE TAUGHT OTHERS TO DO THEM,
AND FURTHERMORE GLADLY COMPLIED WITH THOSE
WHOM I SAW OR HEARD DOING THEM.

ALL SUCH OFFENSES
ARE BOUNDLESS AND LIMITLESS.
AND SO ON THIS DAY, I BRING FORTH GREAT SHAME AND REMORSE.
HONESTLY AND SINCERELY CONFESSING THEM,
I HUMBLY SEEK TO REPENT AND REFORM.

I ONLY HOPE THAT THE TRIPLE JEWEL
WILL COMPASSIONATELY GATHER ME IN;
AND EMIT A PURE LIGHT
THAT ILLUMINES MY PERSON,
SO THAT THE MYRIAD EVILS WILL BE ERADICATED
AND THE THREE OBSTACLES DISPELLED.

MAY I REGAIN THE SOURCE OF MY ORIGINAL MIND,
AND ATTAIN ULTIMATE PURITY!

* * *

FROM BEGINNINGLESS TIME TO THIS PRESENT LIFE,
I HAVE SLANDERED AND DISRUPTED THE TRIPLE JEWEL,
ACTING AS AN ICCHANTIKA
I HAVE DERIDED THE GREAT VEHICLE SUTRAS,
CUT OFF THE STUDY OF PRAJNA,
KILLED MY FATHER AND MOTHER,
AND SHED THE BUDDHA'S BLOOD.

First you should contemplate how from limitless time past, up to the present, you have attempted to destroy the Triple Jewel and have become an icchantika. From limitless kalpas past to the present lifetime, you have slandered and tried to destroy the Buddha, the Dharma, and the Sangha. You have created an infinite number of karmic offenses-- you have been an icchantika. "Icchantika" is a Sanskrit word which translates as "one who does not have faith." They are those who don't believe in the Triple Jewel, and who in the past slandered the Sutras of the Great Vehicle, thereby wiping out their own wisdom. They harmed their parents and slandered the Sutras. They didn't believe in the Sutras. They slandered them by saying, "This Sutra is false and that Sutra is inauthentic." Knowing full well that a Sutra was

spoken by the Buddha, they claimed that it wasn't spoken by the Buddha.
So what is a Sutra spoken by the Buddha and what is not? That which is in accord with principle is a Sutra spoken by the Buddha, and that which is not in accord with principle was not spoken by the Buddha. So, if it accords with principle, then it's a Sutra, and if it doesn't accord with principle, then it's not a Sutra. This is true no matter who spoke the Sutra--whether gods, patriarchs, or Bodhisattvas. You shouldn't think that only if a Buddha spoke a Sutra can you believe it but if a Bodhisattva, a transformation-body spiritual being, or a god spoke it that it's not a Sutra and can't be believed. In fact, all those above-mentioned kinds of beings are qualified to speak Sutras. The only requirement is that what they speak, the doctrines they propound, are correct and in accord with principle.

In the Dharma-ending Age, there are heavenly demons and those of externalist paths who deliberately knit-pick with insignificant, petty questions in an attempt to slander the Sutras of the Great Vehicle. They say, "This Sutra is incorrect and that Sutra wasn't spoken by the Buddha." Since you weren't even born at the time of the Buddha, how can you be so sure about your "facts"? How can you rely on the knowledge and views of an ordinary person to criticize the Sutras? How can you do that?

"A lot of people agree with this opinion." is the comeback. Well, a lot of people don't have any eyes. A lot of people are stupid. They stupidly insist on having their own way and even though they are low and vile, they like to lord it over others. Most of them try to come up with something strange and different in order to make a name for themselves. They try to make it seem as though they really understand things, so they purposely come up with deviant ways of speaking. They say, "This Sutra is 'pure,' but that Sutra isn't backed by proof." They wish to stir up doubts about things. Basically, they're all just messed up and confused, and they haven't any idea what they are talking about. That's what's meant by having "derided the Great Vehicle Sutras."

To "cut off the study of Prajna" means that not only does one not have any wisdom, one also doesn't try to learn to develop genuine wisdom. Without genuine wisdom one becomes more and more stupid, until one commits the Ten Evil Deeds and the Five Reprehensible Acts.

THE TEN EVIL DEEDS

1. killing
2. stealing
3. sexual misconduct
4. greed,
5. hatred
6. stupidity

7. loose speech
8. harsh speech
9. false speech
10. backbiting

THE FIVE REPREHENSIBLE ACTS

1. killing one's father
2. killing one's mother
3. killing an Arhat
4. shedding the Buddha's blood
5. destroying the harmony of the Sangha

Shedding the Buddha's blood includes trying to destroy or harm Buddha images. Destroying the harmony of the Sangha means that one exclusively causes a lot of trouble within the Sangha community by rousing sentiments that are not in accord with the Dharma. These Five Reprehensible Deeds cannot be repented of. Therefore, to commit them is to destroy one's Prajna. One doesn't study wisdom. Having created all these different kinds of karmic offenses, one still doesn't know how to change and repent, and so in the future when one undergoes the retribution, one will fall into the hells.

I HAVE DEFILED THE SANGHARAMA,
BROKEN UP THE PURE CONDUCT OF OTHERS,
BURNED AND DAMAGED STUPAS AND TEMPLES,
AND STOLEN THE SANGHA'S PROPERTY.

"Arama" is a Sanskrit word which means a Way-place. The Way-place is a pure place. It's a place for cultivating. One can defile the Way-place with one's body, with one's mouth, and with one's mind. Defiling the Way-place with one's body refers to making the Way-place filthy through physical deeds. This includes deliberately killing living beings, stealing other's property, engaging in sexual misconduct, indulging in false speech, and taking intoxicants (including drugs and cigarettes). In other words, defiling the Sangharama means breaking the Five Precepts within the Way-place. If one uses one's body to kill living beings, or if one steals things, or if one practices sexual misconduct, or utters false speech, or uses intoxicants in the Way-place, one is defiling the Sangharama with one's body.

Speech is included here because even though one may not commit such acts oneself, if one advocates the committing of all kinds of evil acts with the body, one is responsible for the defiling acts which result. The same is true for advocating the killing of living creatures or acts of stealing, or the use of false speech, or the ingestion of intoxicants. In these cases one is defiling the Sangharama with one's mouth.

As to defiling the Sangharama with one's mind, this occurs when one wishes to destroy the Way-place and thinks up all kinds of tricks and devices to injure the reputation of the Way-place and to destroy and curtail the cultivation and pure conduct of those in the Way-place. For example, one may see people practicing the Dharma-door of Three Steps, One Bow and say, "What merit and virtue is there in doing that?" Instead of praising those cultivators and following along with the merit and virtue, one slanders them. Or perhaps there's a person who is cultivating eating only one meal a day and you prepare things for them to eat at night. That is also destroying the pure conduct of others. One may say things like "There's no merit in cultivating pure practices. This is the Dharma-ending Age and there isn't anyone around who eats only one meal a day. People in the Dharma-ending Age don't cultivate. It's okay to cut corners and do the minimum to get by." If one doesn't praise the cultivation of others, one is just destroying their pure practices.

Or perhaps there are those who cultivate the practice of never lying down and one says, "That's stupid. What use is there in that? See those logs? They just stand up all day, but I haven't seen any of those tree trunks become Buddhas yet." Or one tries to do people in by saying, "What benefit is there in eating vegetarian food? See the cows and horses? They are all vegetarians and I haven't seen any of them attain realization from their cultivation." So one finds all kinds of ways to inject deviant knowledge and deviant views into the minds of people to hamper their cultivation. One tries to undermine the holding of precepts by other people. These are all examples of breaking up the pure conduct of others and of defiling the Sangharama with one's mind. If I were to continue to talk on this subject, there would be a lot more to say.

I have "burned and damaged stupas and temples." Perhaps someone builds a temple and you burn it down out of jealousy, or you burn down pagodas, too. Or you have "stolen the Sangha's property " for your own use. You take the belongings of left home people and convert them to your own personal use. If you do it unintentionally, then it doesn't count. But here it refers to intentional stealing. "Stealing the Sangha's property" means that without getting the permission of the Eternally-Dwelling, you take their property away for your own use. Those kinds of karmic offenses cause people to fall into the hells.

THUS, GIVING RISE TO DEVIANT VIEWS,
I HAVE DENIED CAUSE AND EFFECT.

The greatest obstacle, the greatest fault among cultivators, is to have deviant knowledge and deviant views and not to believe in cause and effect. Deviant views are views that aren't bright and straightforward--they are dark and black. Cultivators who have them take what is true as being false, and they take what's false as being true. They talk about black and do white--they do the opposite of what they say they are going to do. They take what's actually deviant to be proper and what's actually proper to be deviant. Those kinds of people are the dregs of the human race, thieves among the virtuous, demons among those of the Way. They are "weirdos" among humankind. It's very easy for those who cultivate the Way to fall into deviant knowledge and views. If you do fall into deviant knowledge and views, in the future you can become a snake or some other kind of poisonous creature, such as a spider, centipede, or bee--all those kinds of creatures have poison in them. Or maybe you'll become a two-headed snake. If you are very unprincipled in what you do, that is a clear indication that you have all kinds of deviant views--many, many different kinds, not just one.

To "have denied cause and effect " means that you don't believe in the workings of cause and effect. Actually, cause and effect is not off by a hair's breadth, but some people don't believe that. This is especially true of some left-home people. Before leaving the home-life they believed in cause and effect, but after leaving home, they become blasé and don't fear the principle of cause and effect in the least. They become nonchalant, indifferent, and careless.

Why are they not afraid of cause and effect? It's because they have gotten so used to the idea that they simply take cause and effect for granted and think that it's not such a big deal. They no longer believe that when you plant a good cause you reap a good fruit and when you plant an evil cause you reap an evil fruit. Such people don't believe in that principle any longer and they further use all kinds of tricks to oppress, bully, and cheat other people within the Bodhimanda. They make it so that nobody in the Way place is able to cultivate. So that's what is meant by having all kinds of deviant knowledge and views and denying cause and effect.

> I HAVE BEEN INTIMATE WITH EVIL COMPANIONS,
> AND OPPOSED GOOD TEACHERS.
> NOT ONLY HAVE I ENGAGED IN THESE DEEDS MYSELF,
> I ALSO HAVE TAUGHT OTHERS TO DO THEM.
> AND FURTHERMORE, GLADLY COMPLIED WITH THOSE
> I SAW OR HEARD DOING THEM.

One should not draw near to evil teachers. When people who cultivate the Way want to make friends, they should find good friends, not evil ones. What's a good friend? A good friend tells you to cultivate, to hold the precepts, to follow the rules and helps you to cultivate in that way. What's an evil friend? One who tells you not to cultivate but to be lazy and not hold the precepts or follow the rules. Anyone who influences you so that you fall more and more every day is an evil friend. To have deviant views and to flatter people, whooping it up every day, running around together, not following the rules and not holding the precepts, is to be intimate with deviant friends and to oppose your good teacher. A good teacher tells you to hold the precepts, to cultivate and to follow the rules. Evil friends tell you not to follow the rules, not to hold the precepts, and not to cultivate. They're trying to do you in. Opposing one's teacher means not following instructions and not doing what he tells you to do. Your teacher uses up so much of his energy, breath, and blood to teach you and you don't respectfully accord with the rules. That's what's meant by opposing a good teacher. You yourself not following the rules is one thing, but on top of that, you teach others to not cultivate; you don't hold the precepts yourself, and you don't want others to hold them either.

For instance, left-home people can't study the professions of medicine, that is, curing people's illnesses. It's not in accord with the precepts to do so. Fortune telling, such as consulting the hexagrams or using the eight characters, or doing astrology so that one becomes engrossed in talking about what signs particular people are and in doing prognostications from people's physiognomy--all of these activities are impermissible for left-home people to be involved in. Those professions: medicine, fortune telling, astrology, and prognostication are not in accord with the precepts. Therefore, if any of you left-home people have problems in this regard, you should change. You should not study those professions; they are lowly.

You shouldn't make the offenses yourself, nor should you tell other people to do so. Perhaps you see others not following the rules and then you learn from them. You see others not holding the precepts, so you yourself don't hold them. You see others not cultivating the Way and you are influenced so that you don't cultivate the Way either. That's to become "intimate with evil companions" and to end up being corrupted by them. In that way you will definitely fall. So in cultivating the Way, you should definitely draw near to good-knowing friends and leave evil friends alone. You should most certainly not be friends with people who have deviant knowledge and deviant views.

>ALL SUCH OFFENSES
>ARE BOUNDLESS AND LIMITLESS.
>AND SO ON THIS DAY, I BRING FORTH GREAT SHAME AND REMORSE.
>HONESTLY AND SINCERELY CONFESSING THEM,
>I HUMBLY SEEK TO REPENT AND REFORM.

"All such offenses are boundless and limitless," to the point that they can't ever be completely expressed in words. That is why "on this day, I bring forth great shame and remorse." We should all be greatly ashamed and repentant. If you know that you were wrong before, you should quickly change and renew yourself. People who cultivate the Way cannot be greedy about things to eat and then go steal them. They can't be greedy about wearing clothes and want to have more and better clothes than everyone else. Nor should they want to sleep all the time. At all times they must be brave and vigorous. That's the way left-home people should be. Therefore, anyone who is not this way should very sincerely reveal one's faults and repent of them. Hope and pray that the Triple Jewel will compassionately receive your repentance. You have to be very honest and reveal all the faults you have and the mistakes you have made. You have to talk about them all and bring them out in the open. If you aren't true

and sincere and honest, if you are not completely frank when
you repent of your faults and your offenses, then you can't
get rid of them. In everything that you do and in all that
you say, you must use your true mind. You have to speak
sincerely. You shouldn't lie. As soon as you lie, there
will no longer be a possibility for a response to occur.
    This principle applies to people who contact serious
illnesses. If one truly repents, then regardless of the type
of illness, one can get better quickly. But if one protects
and covers over one's faults and refuses to reveal them,
then one's illness will not want to leave one. It's a very
natural and spontaneous kind of thing. If one truly repents
and truly wishes to change, then any illness will get better,
even a fatal one. But in order to have such a response,
one has to truly change. It's not the case that one can
speak falsely and still be able to recover. One must be
ten thousand percent sincere. And one must reveal one's
faults, bring them out into the open, and frankly talk all
about one's offenses and mistakes. One can't have the attitude that one's offenses are too awful and ugly to bring out
into the open and that one can't bear to do so. Don't let
that keep you from revealing them. If you think in that way,
your offenses can't be eradicated. You have to sincerely
seek repentance of all your offense-karma.

> I ONLY HOPE THAT THE TRIPLE JEWEL
> WILL COMPASSIONATELY GATHER ME IN;
> AND EMIT PURE LIGHT
> THAT ILLUMINES MY PERSON,
> SO THAT THE MYRIAD EVILS WILL BE ERADICATED
> AND THE THREE OBSTACLES DISPELLED.
> MAY I REGAIN THE SOURCE OF MY ORIGINAL MIND,
> AND ATTAIN ULTIMATE PURITY!

    Before the Triple Jewel one must speak truly and do true
things, and then there can be an intertwining response, a
true response. So we plead, "'I only hope that the Triple
Jewel will compassionately gather me in.' May they give me
a chance to change my faults and start anew, and may they
'emit pure light that illumines my person.'" The Buddhas
emit a pure, great light which illumines our bodies. When
the Buddhas' pure light shines on us, all our offense karma
is eradicated. All evil is eradicated. None of these exist
any longer. How can they be eradicated? Only through true
repentance. In that way the three obstacles will disappear.
One's karmic obstacles, retribution obstacles, and affliction
obstacles will all disappear. Then one returns to the source

of one's original purity. One returns to one's original face, and obtains ultimately pure happiness.

So no matter who you are, if you have made mistakes and created offenses, you should quickly repent. Offenses that are huge enough to cover the heavens can be wiped away by a single thought of repentance. But if one isn't frank and doesn't repent of them, then it will be difficult for things to improve. It's the mind that enables one to end up in the heavens and it's also because of the mind that one ends up in the hells, or one becomes a hungry ghost or an animal. So it is said,

> *If one wishes to understand*
> *All the Buddhas of the three periods of time,*
> *One should contemplate the nature of the Dharma Realm:*
> *Everything is made from the mind alone.*

It is also said,

> *Offenses arise from the mind*
> *and so they have to be repented of by the mind.*
> *When the mind forgets,*
> *then the offenses are no more.*
> *With mind gone and offenses dispelled:*
> *both are empty.*
> *This is the true repentance and reform.*

Everything is created from our minds. Since offenses are created from our minds, we have to repent with our minds. When our minds forget the offenses, then the offenses are truly banished. When even the thought is forgotten and the offenses are no more, then there is true emptiness. This is called true repentance and reform. This is the method you should use in practicing repentance and reform.

THE JOY OF NOT SEEKING

The less you know about what's going on,
The less affliction you will have.
The more people you know,
The more gossip there will be.

Most people seek knowledge, but cultivators seek "no knowing." Why? Because the less you know about what's going on, the less affliction you will have. If you know just a little, you'll have fewer problems. "The more people you know, the more gossip there will be." Even when there's no gossip, it will start to circulate. Because of this, those who seek learning seek scholastic knowledge, while those who cultivate the Way seek "no knowing."

No knowing just refers to:

Growing up to be a dolt,
One becomes a genius.
Studying until stupid,
One is rare in the world.

When you grow up to be a big dummy, then you're truly sharp. So it is said, "Great wisdom seems like foolishness. Great eloquence seems like clumsy speech." Those who have truly great eloquence seem at a loss for words. They do not talk a lot. They may only say one or two sentences, but they leave everyone else speechless.

"Studying until stupid, one is rare in the world." When you have studied to the point that you seem to be stupid all day, then the miracles can happen; a special state can happen.

It's also said,

When you reach the point that you seek nothing,
Then you have no worries.

That is, in cultivation, you should not seek to become a Buddha, or a Bodhisattva, or to certify to the fourth fruit of Arhatship, or to have great wisdom, or to get enlightened, or to break through your investigation. Don't seek anything. In the very act of seeking, you are adding a head on top of a head; you are riding a donkey looking for the donkey. In cultivation, seek nothing, just cultivate. It's just like eating, wearing clothes, and sleeping. It's a necessity, that's all. You must cultivate every day, day and night the same. That is following conditions, but not changing; not changing, and yet following conditions. You should work in this way and then, when you have reached the extreme point, without seeking enlightenment, you will be enlightened, and without seeking to become a Buddha, you will become a Buddha. Without seeking to become a Bodhisattva, you will certify to the Tenth Ground. So, when the effort takes one to that point, one's success is naturally attained. You don't need to seek. Seeking is just greed; just false thinking.

THE SECRETS OF HEAVEN & EARTH

The secrets of heaven and earth cannot be completely known. When humankind knows all the secrets, the world will cease to exist. It will have to begin all over again. The secrets of heaven and earth: in the small appears the great, and in the great appears the small. Great and small are interfused. So, the Buddha said, "On the tip of a hair appear the kshetras of the Jeweled King. Sitting in a mote of dust is contained worlds to the ends of space and the Dharma Realm. There is not just this one world. There are as many worlds as dustmotes and Buddhas as many as dustmotes. In each world is a Buddha teaching and transforming living beings--this land, that land, and limitless lands; in this world, that world, and all the limitless worlds. What is a world? One Mount Sumeru, one set of the four continents, and one sun and moon make up a world. Ours isn't the only world with a sun and moon. Each world has one of each.
 "Well, why can't I see them?" you say.
 I'll tell you why by way of example. You can see very clearly all the things in the room you are in, but unless you go into the next room, you can't see what's in it. Likewise, we in this world see our sun and moon and continents and know of the Mount Sumeru, but we have never been to other worlds and so we don't see them. It's the same principle. Worlds and everything else as well, speak the Dharma. Everything is alive and growing. The smallest things, like dustmotes, are entities which have their own lives. Great things like Mount Sumerus, have their lives also. Each rock, in fact, is alive and growing. In each rock is the kernal of a small life. The rock's life is very slow and we can't see it with out eyes. Bigger rocks are older than smaller rocks. Rocks can live for several millions or trillions of years.

Trees, grass, and so on, all have life. They are just different forms, and within their lives are more lives still. For example, a tree may contain many bugs in it. People are like this. The human organism is like a big bug, and within our bodies are limitless, boundless small bugs. The small bugs eat the big bug and the big bug eat other things. They are symbiotic and nurture one another in this world.

The earth also has its life. It goes through the process of becoming, dwelling, decay, and extinction for twenty small kalpas each. People are born, get old, become sick, and die. That's another form of birth, dwelling, decay, and extinction. People in the world who have good thoughts increase the good energies. How is the world created? By good thoughts. It dwells in good thoughts. It goes bad when people false think. After it falls apart, it becomes void. So people's thoughts are connected to all living things in the world. Therefore, if people's thoughts are good, the world is peaceful. If people's thoughts are evil, the world is in danger. People should have righteous thoughts and do proper deeds, not be selfish and self-seeking.

Now, in the world, there are so many strange and incurable diseases just because people's minds have gotten too evil. They have created poison in the air and when they breathe it in, their bodies get incurable diseases. Those who study Buddhism must eradicate all the poisons in the world, neutralize them, so they become harmonious energies. Where do the harmonious energies come from? They come about naturally when people stop having afflictions. When the world's energies are harmonious, then people won't be so sick. If everyone is selfish and self-seeking, they will ruin the world.

* * * * *

Dharma Master Sure: I was bowing the other day and contemplating the Avatamsaka Assembly of Buddhas and Bodhisattvas, and I asked myself, "When are you going to become a Buddha?" And the answer was, "As soon as your mind only has Buddha thoughts and no living being thoughts--thoughts of greed, hate, and stupidity. When the mind only has Buddha thoughts, you become a Buddha. Why? Everything comes from the mind. When you have only Buddha thoughts, you are a Buddha."

Ven. Abbot: "What are Buddha thoughts?"

Dharma Master Sure: They start with good thoughts.

Ven. Abbot: If they are good thoughts, why not call them "good thoughts" instead of Buddha thoughts? You say that one with Buddha thoughts is the Buddha, but you don't know what Buddha thoughts are, so you haven't yet become a Buddha.

The thoughts of the Buddha can't be spoken, or thought of.

> *The mouth wants to speak, but words fail.*
> *The mind wants to climb on conditions, but thoughts are gone.*

They are beyond words and all consideration. This describes the time of certifying to the patience with the non-production of dharmas.

I'll mention briefly the Four Aiding Practices of Positions: Heat, Summit, Patience, Foremost in the World. When you start attaining some skill from your cultivation and Ch'an meditation, your body will experience the sensation of heat. It will be filled with heat. This heat melts all illnesses away; also your afflictions. It is like a spring sun which melts away the ice. The heat is *yang*, and is very healthy and vital. So heat is the first stage. Then this heat circulates around your body and rises to the top of your head so that you feel the heat on the summit of your head at all times. That is the second state, Summit. At this time, the pressure becomes very hard to bear, and you can't find ways to relieve the pressure or get the heat out, so you have to be very patient. Therefore, the third stage is called Patience. If you can be patient long enough and keep on applying unstinting effort, then suddenly, you'll make a breakthrough. The "heavenly gate" on the crown of your head will open as the original Dharma body manifests. It swells up filling all of empty space and the Dharma Realm. That level of achievement is known as Foremost in the World, because you're tops with regard to all mundane dharmas. But this doesn't mean that you call yourself number one; rather, the Buddhas and Bodhisattvas recognize and praise such attainment as being number one. Those are the four aiding practices. They are not easy to attain. Cultivation is not easy.

People shouldn't know all the secret profundities in heaven and earth. If you know one thing, you will forget something else. If you know old things, you forget new ones, and vice versa. Because people's brains don't have a lot of vacant space, they can only hold so much garbage. If one tries to put too much in, one's brain gets crammed so full, there's no more room. So if you ask ancient folks about modern things, they don't know, and if you ask modern folks about ancient things, they don't know either. Five thousand years ago, scientists didn't know what they know today. Today's scientists don't know what will be known five thousand years hence. Why? They will forget. It's like a bear in a cornfield. He picks up an ear of corn and stuffs it under his arm and reaches with his other hand to get another, and drops the first one. He goes through a lot of ears of corn, but only ends up with two. Scientists are just like that. You argue that they have books and records, but still, they can't remember that much. They might remember what's in the book they are currently reading, but they will forget the book they just finished. There's nothing new. But things have been forgotten and when they are discovered again, people think they are so incredible and new. Actually, they are really old.

This reminds me, in England there was a person over thirty, and he fell forty feet. He didn't die, but his Heavenly Eye opened. He could see everything within a radius of 100 miles. He could see night and day. He didn't get it through cultivation, and what he did with it was go be a spy for the police. He told them who stole what and where, etc. He would take them right to the spot and find the culprit and evidence. They might deny it but he would relate it down to what pocket they put it in so the police thought he was a treasure worth more than a computer. He solved a lot of cases for them and it's all recorded in Scotland Yard.

If someone thinks, "He opened his Heavenly Eye by falling forty feet. Maybe I'll try that." Don't or you're sure to die. There are inconceivable wonders in this world. There's no way to understand them all. But if you know them all, it's all over, just like when the play is over the curtain falls. If you keep looking to find out what's going on, as soon as you figure out what's going on, it's all over!

Someone asks, "Where is this person? Is he alive or dead? I'd like to see if he can find my diamond ring for me, or my other valuables." Too bad. He's dead. He could see others' things but not his own. One day he went out and perhaps he was so busy looking at things his eyes stuck, and he was killed by a car. So he could see outside things, but didn't know himself--his own life--how it would end. That's a wonder, too: being able to wash others' clothes and yet not knowing his own were dirty; making clothes for other people and yet not having any himself. Things in the world are really inconceivable.

DHARMA-SELECTING EYE

People who learn the Buddhadharma must have the Dharma-Selecting Eye. You must be able to recognize right dharmas and wrong dharmas, black dharmas and white dharmas, good dharmas and evil dharmas. You don't want to take right as wrong and wrong as right, or white as black and black as white. To do that is to be upside down. If you want to recognize these dharmas, you must be replete with the Dharma-Selecting Eye. First of all, you must have no mark of self. Why? Because if you have the mark of a self, you will give rise to all kinds of obstructions. You will be without any wisdom. If you have the mark of a self, then the mind of selfishness will arise. Once the selfish mind manifests, the mind of self-benefitting follows right behind. If you are selfish and self-benefitting, then you will have seeking. If you need to seek after something, then your greed mind is produced. Once the greedy mind is revealed and you can't get what you're seeking, then the mind of contention will arise. You'll always be fighting and contending. But if you can be without a mark of a self, you won't see yourself as so important.

What's meant by the "self"? Ask yourself, "Who am I?" "I am who?" You should investigate the topic "Who is mindful of the Buddha?" The meditation topic if not for reciting. If you only recite it back and forth, it's useless. Instead, you should investigate it, like using a drill to drill a hole. Drilling through and making a hole is likened to obtaining an awakening. When you drill totally through, you become totally enlightened. Then you will understand completely.

Investigate! Don't just try to guess. It's not a guessing game. You can't just speculate about, "I am reciting the Buddha, you are reciting the Buddha, he is reciting the Buddha, and they are reciting the Buddha." You may try to figure it out, back and forth, but you won't get a result that way. Instead, you should look for "who?" The word, "who," is a Vajra Jeweled Sword. It's the wisdom sword. You use this wisdom sword to cut off all other false thinking, so your wisdom will manifest. In the Dharma door of investigating Ch'an, you aren't reciting the topic, "Who is mindful of the Buddha? Who is mindful of the Buddha? Who is mindful of the Buddha?" It's not the same as reciting the Buddha's name. You shouldn't investigate rapidly--that way you recite the Buddha's name. The best thing is to draw out the sound, longer. The word "Who" can be investigated for several hours, even for eighty thousand great kalpas, without your having to cut off your train of thought. That's truly investigating Ch'an. It's a way to truly use the Dharma-Selecting Eye.

Why do we want to investigate "Who?" Originally, the word "who" is also false, but because people are like monkeys, always wanting to find something to do, this method is effective for them. Monkeys look for things to do everywhere, seeking from east to west. People like to be busy too. So we use the word "who" to block other random thoughts so these false thoughts will disappear. This is the Dharma door of "using poison to defeat poison." It is also known as the process of diligently wiping and cleaning. We don't want to let the dust alight. If you can pick up the word "who," then you can use it to wipe away all dharmas and leave all marks. Everything will disappear and be gone.

But if you don't have the Dharma-Selecting Eye, you won't know how to investigate and you will use your effort in vain. You won't be able to recognize the Proper Dharma, but will pursue evil dharmas instead. Like last night, one of my disciples talked. He said that the Asian lefthome people are more compassionate and kinder than American lefthome people. That's a completely erroneous idea. I am from Asia, and I am quite clear about the situation of Buddhism in Asia. There are many phony lefthome people in Asia who seek advantages and who are opportunists. Besides that, I don't see much kindness, compassion, joy, or giving in them. If on occasion, they express joy and giving, they are doing it just to "throw out bricks in hope of attracting jade." And if they seem to be compassionate and kind, they are harboring the thought of climbing on conditions or being obsequious--fawning on people. Their "compassionate" manner is contrived and they harbor ulterior motives. A person who is truly kind and compassionate will not let on; he won't let you recognize him. But if a person wants you to recognize that he is compassionate and kind, he's just playing cat and mouse with you, trying to make friends. That's just psychological trickery; it's phoney. Mind you, not all Asian lefthome people are like this. Some of them have hearts of gold. I'm just saying that there are those who fall into this category and who make a bad name for all of Buddhism.

You yourself don't have the Dharma-Selecting Eye, so you don't recognize what's true and what's false. Don't take a thief as your son. If genuine Buddhism existed in Asia, then it would not have had to come to America to be transmitted here--it would have remained strong in Asia. If you learn crooked and devious ways such as fawning on other people, then even as a lefthome person, you will never attain liberation.

FLAVORFUL CH'AN

When you sit in Ch'an, you should not be greedy for the flavor of Ch'an--the taste of flavorful Ch'an. What does "flavorful Ch'an" mean? It refers to the bliss of the Dhyanas. When you have been sitting just about long enough, you start to experience a feeling of comfort and freedom. When that happens, you may feel kind of indolent--like you don't want to move--you want to just sit there. You become greedy for that feeling of comfort and ease. That's called "flavorful Dhyana." If you become greedy for a state, it's not easy for you to go on and make progress, because you will want to linger there and get attached to that flavorful Ch'an--a state you will keep trying to get back into. You will think, "When am I going to have that kind of a state again? In that state there was no self, no others, no living beings, and no lifespan; no afflictions, and no hassles. It was very, very blissful, very, very comfortable and free. I wonder when I will ever have that experience again." And you will just sit there waiting for that flavorful experience to reoccur. And what happens while you wait? You forget all about applying effort--you are no longer able to do the work.

But people who sit in Dhyana and want to make progress need to be free of any obstructions and be without any hangups. They can't be seeking anything or be greedy for anything. You can't get excessively happy, or depressed, and you shouldn't have any fear or terror. You should see your body as being the same as empty space and as being the same as the Dharma Realm. You don't need to be attached to anything. You don't need to be greedily seeking for anything. Because as soon as you become greedy and seek, you fall into a secondary meaning.

If you keep up with your practice, if you sit long enough, you will reach the Heavens of the First Dhyana. That is also called "the Samadhi of the First Dhyana." The name of the First Dhyana Heaven is "The Ground of Happiness from Separating from Production," so named because there is a happiness which arises from having left behind the afflictions that living beings have from bringing forth the flavor of Dhyana as food and from being filled with Dharma bliss.

At this point you leave behind the confused road of living beings and you start to walk along the road of the Sages which leads to Bodhi. That is the Ground of Happiness of Separation from Production.

Arriving at the First Dhyana isn't something that you can fake; you can't falsely claim, "Well, I have reached the First Dhyana." When you actually arrive at that level there is a sign: your pulse will stop. And you won't have any heartbeat anymore. That is also something which can't be faked. You can't say, "My pulse has stopped!" You couldn't possibly know that. It's something that happens when you enter samadhi. You can't claim, "But I *feel* that it has stopped." How could you feel it? You can only put that over on people who don't know anything about it, people who don't know what gung fu is. If you pretend, you are just trying to sell false goods. But it's not something that you can get away with. However, to talk that much about it will end up obstructing it and so now we are just mentioning a little bit about it in order to keep you from getting devious views and thinking, "I have reached the First Dhyana. I have reached the Joyful Stage of Leaving Production!" In that case, you are just cheating people.

When you have reached the Second Dhyana, you will make even more progress because not only will your pulse stop, but your breath will stop as well. True or false, it isn't something that you yourself would ever be able to claim. There has to be a Good Knowing Advisor who certifies that you have reached that state. And there is a way to prove whether you have done it. It doesn't count just to say you have gotten there. What is the proof? The proof is that you no longer inhale or exhale--your breath has stopped. Yet one has not died; one has just entered the samadhi of the Second Dhyana. You shouldn't think that when you fall asleep you have entered samadhi, because when you are sleeping you are *not* in samadhi. Not only have you not entered samadhi, but when you snore, you have an even louder breath than before, and the people sitting around you hear it as a loud and rumbling thunder. So you shouldn't think that when you have fallen asleep you have reached the Second Dhyana. A cleareyed Good Knowing Advisor can tell as soon as he sees you whether you have reached that state. It isn't a case of your being able to "feel" that it has happened to you. You can't say, "Oh, I don't have any breath!" If you feel you aren't breathing it's just pretense, because basically, you wouldn't know yourself whether you were breathing or not if you were in Dhyana Samadhi. You can't pretend about something like that. You can't put up a false sign and sell counterfeit goods of that kind, because they just won't sell.

Also, this is not the "Second Fruit" (of Arhatship). When you reach the Second Dhyana, it is not a certification, it just means that you have gotten to that place. It's as if you were ultimately going to New York but you have only gone a little ways down the road. So in the Heavens of the Second Dhyana, your breath stops as soon as you enter samadhi.

When you reach the Heavens of the Third Dhyana, your breath has already stopped, and you don't have any heartbeat, and you also don't have any thinking or reflection. The thought processes aren't functioning. The name of the Third Dhyana is, The Ground of Wonderful Bliss of Leaving Happiness Behind. So, the First Dhyana was the Ground of Happiness from Separating from Production, the Second was the Ground of Happiness of the Production of Samadhi, and the Third Dhyana is the Ground of Wonderful Bliss of Leaving Happiness Behind. You don't have even the slightest thought of greed for the samadhis of the First and Second Dhyanas, and there's no attachment to that "flavorful" experience of Dhyana. So that's called the Ground of Wonderful Bliss of Leaving Happiness Behind. And it's a very much higher state than those of the First and Second Dhyanas. All the hairpores on your entire body are blissful at that time. It's as if they were jumping for joy--really, really delighted. However, you don't have any thoughts.

Then, when you reach the Fourth Dhyana, the Ground of Purity of Renouncing Thought, there is nothing at all.

When not a single thought arises, the entire substance manifests.

You don't have even a single thought arise. At that time, it's like when,

For ten thousand miles there are no clouds,
Then there is ten thousand miles of sky.
A thousand pools contain water;
The moon is reflected in all of them.

And when for ten thousand miles there are no clouds, there is ten thousand miles of sky. That's the state that you reach. "Falling flowers and flowing water proclaim the Mahayana." All of them speak Dharma. But that's not a state that you yourself know about. You can't say, "I have reached the state of the Fourth Dhyana," because that would be terrific arrogance on your part. That would be telling a great lie. One must be certified by a clear-eyed, Good Knowing

Advisor. He can tell at a glance just what point your gung fu has reached. And you think, "I think I will go test a Good Knowing Advisor just to see what level I have reached." But if he is a *true* Good Knowing Adivsor, he won't be tested by you and he won't tell you about what state you have reached. So what do you have to do? You have to draw near to a Good Knowing Advisor for a long time. And even when your skill has reached accomplishment, it's not for sure that he is going to tell you. However, it shows in your aura and all one has to do is take a look, because there's a way that it shows and that's how he will know.

A Good Knowing Advisor wouldn't say, "And right now all of us are going to become Buddhas together and go off to a different land." That's really laughable; and it's really pathetic.

THE TRUE WITHIN THE TRUE

(Gold Wheel Temple, Los Angeles. On the occasion of the celebration of the Abbot's Birthday, 1978)

I too wish all of you a Happy Birthday! Whatever day your birthday is, may it be a Happy Birthday. However, I won't say the two words "thank you." I won't thank you, and don't want you to thank me. No one thanks anyone. The ordinary mind is the Way. The straight mind is the Bodhimanda, so we don't need to use polite words. With regard to the Buddhadharma, how should we do things? We should go forward step-by-step and cultivate. For example, the two who are bowing once every three steps have chosen that way to cultivate. In cultivation there are 84,000 Dharma doors. Bowing once every third step is one Dharma door among them. Of those 84,000 Dharma doors, ultimately which Dharma door is number one? Of the 84,000 Dharma doors, 84,000 are number one. What does this mean? It means, if the Dharma suits your potentials, then it's the number one Dharma. If it doesn't suit your potentials, then it is not number one for you. However, if it doesn't suit your potentials, it may suit someone else's potentials. Any Dharma that suits anyone's potentials is number one for that individual. Therefore, they are all number one Dharma doors; all are non-dual Dharma doors. If you try to force a discrimination of which is best and say, "This one is number one, that one is number two, and then there are the third, the fourth, counting up to 84,000," no one would cultivate the 84,000th Dharma door. Why not? Because it's the very last one. The way that people's minds work is that they want to be number one. Therefore, I don't pay any attention to whether it's right or not; I just call all the Dharma doors spoken by the Buddha "number one," without any number two. Whether you take a logical, psychological, philosophical, or scientific stance, all are number one. All are part of the 84,000 Dharma doors. The same applies to each one of us. Each person is number one. There is no number two. For there to be a number two, you would have to tie two people together.

You say, "Now I understand! Now that you've spoken this Dharma, Dharma Master, I have opened Enlightenment. What enlightenment have I opened? When a man and woman marry, that counts as number two!" Not bad. Not only number two, it's even number three. A third one also appears. So it would go, all the way up to 84,000. But if you don't count that way, then all are number one. Every single one is number one. Why should each one be number one? It's because every person wants to be number one. No one wants to be number two. Even the most stupid person considers himself number one, "All of you take a look: not one of you is as stupid as I am! I'm number one in stupidity!!" However, he himself doesn't admit that he's number one in stupidity. He still feels he's smarter than anyone else. So didn't Mencius say:

> *People all say, "I have wisdom." But if you trap them in either a fishnet or a pitfall, they don't even know enough to get out of it.*

So how could they be said to have wisdom? While we are in the world, whatever we do, it's all a part of empty space, and all a portion of the Dharma Realm. Therefore, trying to be number one is an attachment on the part of people: one attaches to oneself being better than other people and says, "I'm number one in the entire world." Take a look. No matter who it is, everyone feels he is better than everyone else. No one really admits, "I don't match up to other people." Not one. You may say, "Well, so and so is really courteous." They are just being polite, and it's not for sure in their mind they admit to being inferior to other people. All of you think it over. Although I haven't obtained a PH.D. in Psychology, I still understand about people's minds. Almost everyone thinks that he himself is fantastic. If someone praises him he doesn't stop to think, "Is that the case or not?" "Is it true or false?" Most people don't think that way. How do they think? They think, "They said I'm number one: it's certain that I'm number one." That is the way most people are; people who study the Buddhadharma should have no self, and not seek to be "number one." One should be without a self.

> *When one succeeds in becoming a great fool,*
> *One is an outstanding person.*
> *If one studies to the point of being as if stupid,*
> *One is rare in the world.*

If a person becomes someone who seems to have no sense or wisdom, he is exceptional and wonderful. If one studies to the point of being like a fool who sits there not thinking south, not thinking north, not thinking east, not thinking west, not thinking of ascending to the heavens and not thinking of descending to the earth, then one is rare in the world. To watch over things on the outside is easy. To watch over inner matters is what's not easy. Outside matters are, for instance, being manager of such and such a corporation, and having a large number of people in one's jurisdiction. One may manage people but one is unable to manage the false thoughts in one's own mind. One may tell them not to come up, but if this one does not come up, that one appears. One keeps thinking things like, "There's going to be a party. Do I want to go to that party or not? I should go to the party. It's at 7:30. I should get there at 7:20." One's false thoughts keep arising. If one says, "You don't have to think; I'll just get there and let it go at that," it won't do. One has to think. One has to have a plan-- an advance course of action. You see? Having a party is that way, and so is going to the movies, even to the point that when watching television at home it's, "Oh, *that* program is on. Do I want to turn the television on and look at it?" Not to speak of adults, even the children have gotten caught up in this. They turn on the television and watch it for hours. See? No one taught them how, yet they are able to do it. That's all speaking Dharma.

In the world, all the myriad existing things are speaking Dharma. If you understand, they are speaking Dharma. If you don't understand and think instead that they're a lot of fun, then you'll end up being confused by them. If you are confused by them, then you won't be able to awaken. You'll be as if asleep. When you sleep, you don't know anything at all. When you wake up, you know you've been asleep; before you wake up you don't know. People who study the Buddhadharma to the point of understanding, are also that way. They are as if asleep when they are muddling around being people, either thinking of getting rich, or thinking of holding public office, or thinking of becoming a celebrity, or thinking of fame and profit. They think these things are all a lot of fun, really fine, and will bring happiness. Then, when the time comes, the Ghost of Impermanence arrives and everything's over, everything's gone, and you say, "Oh! If only I had known it was going to turn out like this, then I would not have been so attached! I would have understood a little better and opened a little wisdom." Then there won't be any more time; it will be too late.

> *Don't wait until you're old to cultivate the Way:*
> *Many are the solitary graves of young people.*

See how many solitary graves there are? All of those are young people. Old people have their sons and daughters along with them. That doesn't hold nowadays, however, in the public cemetaries. Daughters can't even find their own fathers because they aren't put together. So, the world is changing, and every single thing is speaking the Dharma of changing and transforming. What are the changes and transformations for? They are to get people to wake up; and they are to confuse people. How do they confuse people? They are confusing if people don't understand the true principle behind them. When that happens, people become more and more confused each day. How do they wake people up? If people understand the Dharma that everything is speaking, they can awaken to the fact that everything in the world is impermanent.

> *Blessings and honor are springtime dreams,*
> *And fame, a single floating cloud.*
> *The flesh and bones before your eyes are*
>   *no longer true;*
> *Love and affliction turn to enmity and*
>   *hate.*

Look at how many men and women start out in love--they love and love--but then they experience a change of heart and the pain is unbearable. Love turns to hate.

> *Don't burden your neck with golden armor,*
> *Don't bind your body in a prison of jade.*
> *With a pure mind and few desires cast*

off the red dust:
Happiness and bliss are basic to us all.

If you are able to understand this principle, then you won't be attached to anything at all. If you can be without attachments, then you'll be relaxed. If you are relaxed, then you can attain liberation. What's meant by attaining liberation? It just means having no afflictions. Having no afflictions is liberation. If you have afflictions, it's as if you were tied up.

All of you have come here today, yet the weather is very hot, and there's a lot of smog, and I didn't have any good things to give you to eat. Basically, the rice and vegetables that were handed out were brought by other people. All I can do is speak some it's-not-known-whether-true-or-false, Dharma. If all of you feel it suits you, then use it. If I say more, it won't be of any great use. You should just have no afflictions, no attachments. Take things more lightly. Don't see life as so weighty. Don't take things so seriously. In your mind constantly wake up. Wake up to the fact that everything is impermanent. There's a verse that expresses this well:

This day is already done.
Our lives are that much less.
We're like fish in a shrinking pond;
What joy is there in this?

We should be diligent and vigorous,
As if our own heads were at stake.
Only be mindful of impermanence,
And be careful not to be lax.

This day is already done. This day has already gone by. *Our lives are that much less.* Our life is that much shorter. *We're like fish in a shrinking pond.* It is just like a fish in water which is daily drying up. Since the water the fish is in is getting less and less each day, what happiness would you say the fish had? The day of his death is not far off. We are not unlike that fish. *What joy is there in this?* What bliss is there in this?

We should be diligent and vigorous, as if our own heads were at stake. Therefore, we should be as diligent as if someone wanted to cut off our heads. If that were really the case, we would certainly try to find a way to protect our heads. *Only be mindful of impermanence, and be careful not to be lax.* We should always think about how, in the future, the Ghost of Impermanence will come to drag us off. In that way, we will not fail to follow the rules.

At all times you should hold the precepts. Don't tell lies; don't always have a phony face mask on. What you do should be *true*. You should have a true heart, a true mind. Be true upon true. You should become the true within the true. Therefore, four or five years ago at the City of Ten Thousand Buddhas, I said, "You can search the entire world and you'd never find one thing that's true." Then Kuo Chen's ("True"), eyes opened wide and he stared at me open-mouthed. "Oh?' his meaning was, "I'm right here in front of you and you can't find me?" However, it was because he was there that I said it. If he hadn't been there, I wouldn't have talked that way. So, do you understand? That's what I said four or five years ago. Now these two who have been bowing once each third step have been working for one year now. Today is exactly the date--it just happened to work out right.

Today too, is the first of the fourth month, and it's the one-year anniversary of the beginning of the pilgrimage of the two who are bowing every third step. I'm not jealous today that all these people have not come for my birthday-- they've come for the anniversary of you two who are bowing every third step!

STICKY LOVE

(The Abbot holds up the famous tree trunk).

This is the remains of two separate tree trunks, but the upper parts and lower parts are stuck together. I will tell you the story behind this piece of tree trunk.

A long time ago there was a man and a woman who were very much in love. Together they made these vows, "In heaven may we be like birds tied together to the same wing and on earth may our roots intertwine." This vow took place many aeons ago, one knows not how many. It was love at first sight when these two people met. They had the same hobby: money. The man did whatever he could to earn the money, and the woman did her best to spend it, and they were really busy at the game of bringing in the money and cashing out. But they were so much in love and engrossed in each other that their karma got deeper and deeper until they fell into the realm of the animals, then into the realm of the hungry ghosts, and then into the realm of hell beings; and after a long time they finally became grass and trees. In this particular instance, this piece of wood was originally two separate tree trunks, but now they are hopelessly intertwined. The man is grasping at the woman and the woman is hugging the man--they are tied together in embrace. They have a little stone stuck between them and they cherish it as their diamond; it's their joint account book from past lives. So you can see that they are still as muddled in the vegetable kingdom as they were in the human one.

One spring day several years ago, at the City of Ten Thousand Buddhas, we went to the river to speak the Dharma and found this piece of wood. The top of these tree trunks have been chopped off and the roots have also been severed, but still these two are entangled in an embrace. Wouldn't you say this is pitiful? Look really closely now--study it really carefully. This is a case of loving too deeply and it's really dangerous! It's not all fun and games.

Someone might be having this false thought. "It's well that you tell this story, but how can we really believe it? What proof do you have to back it up? There's no logic at all behind it. Probably you are putting us on as if we were children. It's just dream talk." Well you don't have to believe it and I don't have to force you, because this Dharma is very difficult to understand and accept, even when one knows it's true. That's because once people fall in love they can get very confused and fall so deeply in love that no mat-

ter what others may say, they won't buy it. It's very difficult to give up love and cultivate the Way. There's a saying in Chung Wen,

> He holds on to a dried turd and if you try to give him a delicious donut, he won't relinquish the turd for the donut.

With such an attachment I can't help you break through it. So it's said,

> Although the Dharma rain is abundant,
> It is impossible to nourish those who don't have any roots.
> Although the Buddha-door is wide,
> It's impossible to take across those who don't have faith.

    I have kept this piece of wood for a long, long time now and have taken really good care of it. When visitors come I don't just casually show it to them, because most people won't believe it, and even if you tell them this dharma they won't believe. So most of the time I just choose not to mention it. However, I brought this piece of wood to the Buddhahall over three weeks ago, and every day hence I've wanted to tell you this story, but the conditions weren't right, so I didn't talk about it. But I see that more and more people are heading for home so I may never get another chance if I don't tell you about it now. So today I don't care whether you believe or not; I have told you this story. Now that I have explained to you about the causes and conditions of this piece of wood, you can choose for yourselves whether or not to accept it and understand it.

* * *

    As to this public record I just told you, if you choose not to believe it, that's okay, but what I am now about to tell you is 100% fact and you absolutely must believe it. Why do people study the Buddhadharma? It is in order to separate from suffering and leave death. How unfortunate that though they may want to get out of confusion, people get immersed right in confusion! So, although their original intent is to get out of suffering and attain bliss, with a single false thought they can easily fall into a trap. If one isn't careful and doesn't use the Dharma selecting eye, one can easily get deluded and be led astray by people with deviant knowledge and views. These people couldn't really expose themselves to the public because then they would completely lose face. When a mute person eats golden seal he knows how bitter it is, but he can't say anything. What do I mean? People start out wanting to leave desire, but they run right smack into the pit of desire, so that right within the Buddhadharma there are a lot of impure relationships; that it goes on and on in a big, stinking mess, and you can't tell anyone about these things--it's too shameful. That's a case of the confused leading the confused and it's really very sad. They bore right into the hells together.

I can't go on because this subject is just too painful. But I must tell you one more thing. In the so-called "secret schools" they mantra back and forth and tell you that men and women can cultivate together and reach the highest ecstasy--coupling together--they say it's truly out-of-sight, because while releasing their desire they can at the same time become Buddhas in this very life. Impossible!!! It simply can't be done!!! With deviant views like that they think they have found a way to liberation. But when they die they bore right into the hells. The "secret school"-- secret, secret, secret, until they end up in the wombs of animals and that's just how secret they get. What I am saying is not the slightest bit overstated. And I am certainly not scolding or bad-mouthing people. But we'll leave that aside and now I want to discuss with you an even bigger problem--homosexuality.

This problem alone turns people around so that they are not even living beings anymore. Most of them aren't even up to being ghosts or animals. This problem turns heaven and earth upside down. It goes against anything that is principled. It's a case of demons and freaks fanning the flames and engaging in this practice and going straight for the hells. In this world, men and women getting married is a very natural thing, and if you don't mind following along with the natural cycle of birth and death, that's what you would do--get married to one of the opposite sex. But homosexuality contradicts human obligations and heavenly propriety--it contradicts biological principles, natural principles and spiritual principals--all those aspects. One of the retributions for this practice is to be born as a siamese twin--babies with their bodies or limbs stuck together-- or even as siamese animal twins. You will see this happen more and more now because there are so many homosexuals around. So, if someone doesn't know about the Buddhadharma and doesn't understand the Buddhadharma, his or her offenses could still be excusable. But if you understand the principles of cause and effect, then you should review what I've said tonight very clearly and very carefully, and make sure you don't go down the wrong road.

PRECEPTS, SAMADHI AND WISDOM

*Diligently cultivate precepts, samadhi and wisdom;
Put to rest greed, hatred, and stupidity.*

   Diligently cultivating precepts means putting a stop to evil and avoiding wrong-doing. It is also doing no evil but offering up all good. It means when you recognize your true and actual goal, you should go forward and make courageous progress with vigor, and not change your initial resolution. It also means that you should be firm, sincere, and constant. Your resolve should be solid and firm, it should be sincere, and it should be long-lasting. Constantly and forever one should do no evil and should offer up all good conduct. When you cultivate precepts, you certainly must have patience. That is, you must endure what you cannot endure. In that way the precepts will spontaneously be pure. When the substance of the precepts is pure, then you will be able to give rise to samadhi-power. Samadhi power means not being moved by outer circumstances. What is meant by wisdom? People with wisdom don't do stupid or upside-down things. They don't do ignorant and afflicted things. That's wisdom.
   If you can diligently cultivate precepts, samadhi, and wisdom, and in turn, put to rest greed, hatred, and stupidity, then in everything you say and do, you won't calculate for yourself. You should consider the entire world and all of humanity as your responsibility and be concerned about them. Don't be concerned about yourself, and then you won't have any greed. If you make all of humanity your personal responsibility, and set out to benefit each and every person, then you are practicing the Bodhisattva Path. If further, you can have no stupidity and afflictions, then your hatred will be put to rest. Stupidity means not recognizing truth and instead doing all kinds of deluded things. If you have no more of all that, then you have put to rest greed, hatred, and stupidity.
   Within the Buddhadharma, you can talk about it forwards and backwards, but it never gets beyond precepts, samadhi and wisdom; greed, hatred, and stupidity. If you can dili-

gently cultivate precepts, samadhi and wisdom, then that's a case of "a superior person ascending." If you are unable to diligently cultivate precepts, samadhi, and wisdom, and cannot put to rest greed, hatred, and stupidity, then that's a case of "a petty person descending." Therefore, ascending and descending are right within a single thought. If we know something is not right, then no matter what, we should not do it. If we know something is right, then no matter how difficult it is, still, we should find a way to do it. Because we are studying the Buddhadharma, we should never be lax. It doesn't matter where we are, on every path and byway, we should diligently cultivate precepts, samadhi, and wisdom and put to rest greed, hatred, and stupidity. We should never be lax. Therefore, while on the bus we continue to hold lectures and continue to have morning and evening recitations.

Further, don't pay any attention to whether there are any advantages to cultivation--just cultivate. Don't pay attention to whether you can become enlightened or not, whether or not you can obtain some benefits, perhaps open up your wisdom. Just cultivate. It should be just like eating: don't pay any attention to whether eating food meets particular nutritional requirements of our body. Just eat things to help your body stay alive. That's why you eat. Cultivation helps keep the wisdom-life of our Dharma body alive, and so we cultivate. Therefore, if you want to get enlightened and want to become a Buddha, you still have greed. You shouldn't be seeking anything.

> *When you reach the point of no seeking,*
> *Then you have no worries.*

If you seek something, then you have afflictions. If you weren't seeking something, then what afflictions would you have? All of you think it over. You should pay particular attention to this point: if you were not seeking anything, then what afflictions would you have? Afflictions just come from your seeking something. When you don't get what you seek, you become afflicted. When you don't get what you want, you suffer, and after you've been suffering for awhile, then you cry. After having cried, then you start to get angry. After getting angry, you end up in jail! So you should have no self. If you had no self, then why would you want to get enlightened? Why would you want to become a Buddha?

In bowing once every third step, one is bowing in empty space, riding the clouds and driving the fog--not seeking anything; not even world peace!

DON'T HAVE FOX DOUBTS

If you want to end birth and death, you cannot be afraid of being lonely. You have to cut off desire and love. Even though some people aren't really confused about this, they still don't want to put down desire and love.

You can repay the kindness of your teacher by not losing your temper, by not having any fire, and by not getting angry. I only wish for one thing: that my disciples will not have any temper. "But you have a temper," you say. Yes, but I can take everyone else's temper. I can be scolded and not answer back. I can be patient with insult. When I was a novice in Chung Kuo, the elder left-home people scolded me right and left, and even the younger left-home people scolded me--I was the runt. I got the brunt of it. And that's what I owe my success to today.

I cannot really speak the Buddhadharma, nor can I propagate the Buddhadharma--all I can do is speak some very plain and honest words. I don't use flowery speech or elegant sentences to try and cheat you. I just want to teach you the Dharma. I can only tell you today, how not to be a fox immortal.

There was once an elder Bhikshu whom someone asked, "Do great cultivators fall in accordance with cause and effect?"

The elder cultivator replied, "Great cultivators do not fall in accordance with cause and effect." Because that one sentence was incorrect, he had to undergo rebirth as a fox for five hundred lives. When Ch'an Master Pai Chiang was at Chinag Hsi lecturing the Sutras, there was an old man with a long beard who came to listen every day. No one knew who he was. He always left as soon as the lecture was over. The lectures were open to the public, of course, so no one asked him who he was; he was free to come and go with everyone else. In lecturing Sutras, the rule is for the Dharma Master to return to his room immediately after he finishes lecturing. He should engage in conversation very rarely, lest he end up seeking advantage from conditions. He should not linger after the lecture in order to invite people to come back again, or the like. One day, when Ch'an Master Pai Chiang was returning to his quarters after the lecture, the old man with a long beard followed him and asked for instruction. His question was, "Does a great cultivator fall in accordance with cause and effect?"

Ch'an Master Pai Chiang answered, "Great cultivators are not unclear about cause and effect." At that, the old man immediately became enlightened.

"Oh, so that's the way it is!" he exclaimed. Then he explained, "I am a fox who lives on the mountain behind here. Every day I come to listen to the Sutras, but I've never understood this principle." Then he explained that in the past he had been a high monk who had also lectured the Sutras, but when someone had asked him that question, he had answered incorrectly, and as a result, had to undergo five hundred lives as a fox. "Now that today I have finally understood, tomorrow I will go be reborn. You could come back to my cave and bury my corpse in order to establish affinities."

The next day, Ch'an Master Pai Chiang, taking all the monks from the monastery with him, went back on the mountain to have a look. Sure enough, they found the corpse of an old fox. Ch'an Master Pai Chiang buried it with the ceremony used for monks, and crossed him over.

I don't have spiritual penetrations because I am not a fox spirit. Being too clever can really do you in. If you are too clever, you could be off by just a hair and fall and become a fox. So, anyone who thinks they want to be a fox can just be casual about answering questions put to them.

WHEN PEOPLE DON'T LIKE YOU

In cultivating the Way, sometimes you may find that you are unable to find the Path, that you don't know how to go about cultivating. You may run into a fork in the road and you don't know which way to go. At that time you need to have wisdom and samadhi power. You must also hold the precepts.

As to relationships with people, sometimes you may be especially good to some people, but they return your kindness with dislike. The better you are to them, the worse they will be to you. When this state manifests, you must break your attachment. What attachment? Your attachment to being good to people! When the better you are to people the worse they are to you, they are being your "reverse" good knowing advisors. They are helping you learn to take it easy when the going gets rough. This is based on experience in my own cultivation. At every step along the way, I have encountered these types of abuse and these sorts of tests. Abuse and tests occur just to see whether you will still go forward or whether you'll retreat. If you really understand, then in opposing and according states you will be equally vigorous. There is a saying:

> If your ideas aren't working,
>   look within yourself;
> If you are kind to people and they
>   don't reciprocate, take a look at
>   your kindness.
> If you give people orders and they don't
>   follow them, take a look at
>   your orders.
> If you pay respect to people and they
>   don't return it, take a look at
>   your manners.

Suppose you are very good to someone, but they won't get near you. In that case, you have to return the light to see if your kindness is really adequate. If it is, eventually you will influence them towards the good. If people don't follow your instruction, return the light and think, "Could I be laying power trips on people? If you nod or do a half-bow when you see people, but they act as if they didn't even see you, once again, return the light: Do you really feel respectful towards them? If you can always return the light, you won't be too far away from the Path. You'll be on your way. This is very easy to talk about but very difficult to do!

NEWS FROM CHINA: THE FIVE EYES

For the past thirty years, Buddhism in China has been obstructed by the Communists. You could say that for these past thirty years, there has been no Buddhism in China. Many Buddha and Bodhisattva images in the temples there were smashed or otherwise destroyed, particularly during the Great Cultural Purge. At that time, the Buddhas no longer emitted light, the Bodhisattvas did not speak, and the Arhats just entered samadhi. The Little Red Guards had no fear in their hearts. They went about wreaking havoc in all the temples and monasteries, particularly those at the Four Holy Mountains (dedicated to the Four Bodhisattvas: Manjushri, Universal Worthy, Kuan Yin and Earth Store). Although it's said that the Buddhas and Bodhisattvas entered samadhi, didn't emit light, and didn't speak, after a while they couldn't take it any more, so they sent some people who had made great vows in the past to China to renovate Buddhism. Those people took along with them some spiritual powers--specifically, the Five Eyes:

1) The Heavenly Eye
2) The Buddha Eye
3) The Wisdom Eye
4) The Dharma Eye
5) The Flesh Eye

These Five Eyes are different from the ordinary eyes of people. The Flesh Eye among the Five Eyes does not refer to a flesh eye in the physical sense of the word. This Flesh Eye can perceive objects that have shape and form and that is why it takes the name "flesh"--referring to what it can see.

At the present time there are some children in Mainland China who can "see" things. The authorities in China don't say that they can "see," however; they claim these children "hear" things. The scientists, philosophers, and neurologists in China can be said to be, "brewing tea with cold water," because they pretend to understand what this matter is all about. They say that those children can "hear" words from afar. But in fact this ability is not a function of "hearing" but rather of "seeing." If the scientists write down certain words on a piece of paper and place the children some distance from the words, the children can "see" those words. Before they can do this, however, they must become absorbed for a moment in stillness and concentration. But just because they close their eyes when they do this, the scientists assume that the children "hear" rather than "see" the words. Actually, during this time, they close their ordinary eyes, but open their Five Eyes. When their Five Eyes are opened, the children can see everything all around them very clearly. That is how they are able to see the words at a great distance.

It's illogical to say that they "hear" the words, anyway, because words written on paper don't emit sounds. They have no frequency. If they don't emit sounds, how can they be "heard"? It is truly a regrettable state of affairs that in a country which has twelve billion people, no one understands the principle of the Five Eyes! Even though they have among them so many scientists, philosophers, and neurologists, nobody really knows what's going on. It's rumored that there are over a thousand of these children presently under intensive scrutiny by the scientists. However, it's to be feared that the more the scientists investigate, the farther removed from the truth they will become. Why? Because they don't understand the principle of the Five Eyes. What a shame! A country as large as China and nobody understands!

"Do people in other countries understand?" you wonder.

No, they are puzzling over it too, craning their necks and speculating, wondering what's going on. Nobody is endowed with true knowledge and far-reaching insight. Ultimately, where can you find people who really understand true principle?!

* * *

SCIENCE: BOON OR BANE?

Science absolutely cannot bring about true or ultimate happiness to people--neither spiritually nor materially. This is something which most people will find hard to accept. Why? Because people are too involved in their attachments and do not wish to relinquish them and thereby awaken to higher truths. Anyone who is an exponent of the principle I have just stated is bound to be considered a loser. The lure of scientific and material progress is stronger than any other force. Fully aware of the flaws within science, people still flock to the scientific point of view--that's how great the attraction is.

You should know, however, that in this world the beneficial aspects of anything are always countered by their harmful aspects. To whatever extent something is beneficial, it is equally harmful. Cancer, for instance, is becoming more and more wide-spread. This disease is a direct result

of scientific progress. Toxic vapors which are by-products
of new scientific inventions saturate the air. People
breathe this air and come down with all sorts of bizarre illnesses. Is it the case that the scientists are oblivious
to this fact? Most likely not. They probably are aware of
it, but they don't want to admit it or confront the issues
involved. The situation is already critical--nearly termi-
nal--almost beyond redemption. Yet although it is beyond
practical hope, we still have to do as much as we are able.
That doesn't mean one must protest against science. Instead,
you should thoroughly understand the principle that for every
benefit there is an equal amount of harm.

Another example is our ability to go to the moon. What
if people decide to stockpile hydrogen bombs there, so that
if they explode they will wipe out all of humanity? What
if one of those bombs were to go off and destroy the moon?
Then there'd be no more moon. Can you imagine what the
world would be like without a moon? This is just an example,
but you can get the idea.

The more advanced science becomes, the more in danger
become the lives of people. This sort of "progress" is
tantamount to deliberately ingesting poison. In the past
when there were no technological advancements, people were
quite content and comfortable. But in the present age, with
its myriad "inventions," people become stricken with all
sorts of weird diseases and unexplainable fatal illnesses.
In imperceptible ways, these incurable diseases are being
created by science.

> If there is good, there is also bad;
> If there is benefit, there is also harm;
> If there is success, there is also
>   failure.

This describes our world of relative, not absolute, dharmas.

* * *

...ON THE SHURANGAMA MANTRA

In investigating the Shurangama Mantra, you must first
of all be unselfish. You shouldn't have the thought of self-
benefit, either. You should have an unselfish mind and
great regard for the public's welfare--a straight and proper
mind, an impartial mind. You should have a mind of self-
sacrifice for the sake of others. Your thoughts should be
those of universally crossing over all living beings. If
you're able to bring forth this type of mind, then in your

study of the Shurangama Mantra, you will quickly attain accomplishment.

This section of the Mantra is primarily concerned with the Dharma of Hooking and Summoning. It hooks and summons the heavenly demons and those of outside ways, draws them to this Way-place, and tames and subdues them. There are five Dharmas at work in this Mantra:

1) The Dharma of Hooking and Summoning
2) The Dharma of Taming and Subduing
3) The Dharma of Eradicating Disasters
4) The Dharma of Increasing Benefit
5) The Dharma of Accomplishment

People at the City of Ten Thousand Buddhas should maintain a mind of benefitting other people in every thought. If the opportunity doesn't present itself, of course, there is no way to benefit others; but if there's a chance to do so, then you should help people. If you can be this way, then all the Dharma-protecting good spirits will protect you. But if you speak this way and yet your mind works the opposite way, then all the Dharma-protecting good spirits, all the gods, dragons, and the rest of the eight-fold division of ghosts and spirits, will stay far away from you. None of them will protect you. Way-virtue must be emphasized in the minds of all those who live at the City of Ten Thousand Buddhas. This means you shouldn't hurt, hinder, harm, or obstruct people in your thoughts. Don't get in the way of others. It shouldn't be that your words ring true but your thoughts have falseness in them. Don't have a false mind behind a true mouth. Your words and thoughts cannot contradict each other.

The straight mind is the Bodhimanda.

At all times you must use a straight mind.

* * *

THESE SIMPLE VERSES:
THE SHURANGAMA MANTRA

For a hundred, thousand, myriad aeons, no one has explained the Shurangama Mantra, even once. It's not easy to lecture on it, even once. I am lecturing on it for you now, but it's not for sure any one of you understands it. Some may *feel* they understand it, but not *really* understand it.

Some may feel they already understand it and so not pay attention, but that's just the same as not understanding at all. The Shurangama Mantra has a force that upholds heaven and earth and keeps them from becoming extinct. It is that spiritual force which prevents the world from coming to an end. I have said that as long as one person can recite the Shurangama Mantra, the world won't be destroyed and the Dharma won't become extinct. When there's not a single person left who can recite the Shurangama Mantra, the Buddhadharma will die out.

Heavenly demons and those of outside ways are now spreading rumors that the *Shurangama Sutra* and Mantra are inauthentic. They are simply demon sons and grandsons sent by heavenly demons and those of outside ways to spread such rumors so as to destroy people's faith in the Shurangama Mantra. If no one believes in the Mantra, then no one will recite it. When no one recites it, the world will quickly be destroyed. Therefore, if you don't want the world to be destroyed, then study and practice the Shurangama Mantra; read and recite the Shurangama Mantra. If you can recite it every day, then in this threatening nuclear age the dangers of nuclear power will not affect you. Therefore, we should single-mindedly read and recite the Shurangama Mantra.

I am now lecturing the Shurangama Mantra for you, but it's not necessarily the case that anyone understands it yet. Maybe in ten, eighty, a hundred, or a thousand years from now someone will come across this very shallow commentary on the Shurangama Mantra and gain deep understanding from it. You who get to hear these Shurangama Mantra lectures shouldn't think it's such an easy thing to do. Although these four-line verses are very shallow they flow forth from my heart and my nature. They are definitely not plagiarized from any other book or commentary. When you follow me in studying this, don't worry about whether the verses are good or not. I have written these verses according to my point of view and my understanding of the meaning of the Shurangama Mantra. If you really want to understand the Shurangama Mantra, then you should pay close attention and study. Don't let this time go by in vain.

CONCENTRATION

In cultivation, knowing ten parts is not as good as practicing one part. So, those who study the Dharma shouldn't know too much. If you know too much you will just get confused. You won't know which Dharma door to pick. Concentrating on one Dharma door is the best. For example, kids who know how to cry should cry. Those kids who can laugh, should laugh. That's "concentration." Those who know how to bow to the Buddha should concentrate on bowing to the Buddha. Those who know how to recite Sutras should recite Sutras. Those who like to recite mantras should just recite mantras. Those who like to lecture should look into how others lecture, and gain fluency.

> *If you concentrate, it is efficacious.*
> *If you get scattered, the effort is lost.*

Concentrate. Do not get scattered. If you put your mind to it, you can accomplish anything. If a doctor concentrates, he can cure all of his patients. When concentrating, intent on one's altruistic aims, and resolved to relieve humankind of its suffering, one is sure to cure them successfully. This is singleminded concentration. If you don't concentrate and think, "I don't care if they are sick, as long as I get my money," that's not concentrating. No matter what one's occupation is and no matter how rich one is able to get, one should not forget about doing merit and virtue. If one doesn't do merit and virtue, one will not be able to cultivate and thus not be able to become a Buddha. If one doesn't have merit and virtue, then although one may get rich, one won't be able to hold on to one's wealth. Some disaster will strike and one will lose everything. Therefore, one must stress virtue. For every part of merit one does, one obtains ten parts reward. For every 10% investment, one gains a 100%. First one must do more merit and virtue. That is why people say,

> *You search the mountain for the highest energy source.*
> *Who would have guessed that it's the square inch?*

The "square inch" is just the mind. So no matter what people do, they can't separate from merit and virtue.

You may say, "But nowadays, no one talks about virtue or righteousness. People who know how to take what they want are all doing quite well, whereas those who emphasize merit and virtue take more and more of a loss each day." You should know that those who are doing well cultivated in former lives. It's not that if you do good in this life you will get your reward right off. If you are straightforward, you might get your reward this life. If you aren't straight on, you'll have to wait till next life to get your reward. So no one should think that you can figure out what's really happening just by looking at what you see right in front of you. If someone is unprincipled but still doing well, it's because he or she prepared the ground in past lives and is now enjoying the fruits. If you prepare now, in future lives you will receive your reward. The *Sutra on the Cause and Effect of the Three Periods of Time* says,

> *Why is someone wealthy in this life? It is because in past lives they made offerings to the Sangha and helped the poor. Why is one poor in this life? It is because one didn't give to the poor in former lives. Why is someone handsome in this life? It is because in past lives they made offerings of flowers and incense and lamps before the Buddha.*

Why is it that someone has so many affinities with people and no one dislikes them? It's because they made offerings of lamps and candles and incense in front of the Buddha. From this we know that what we are now undergoing depends on what we did in the past. What we will be in the future depends on what we do right now. That's how things work.

TURN AFFLICTIONS INTO BODHI

March 31, 1978
Gold Wheel Temple, L.A.

DISCIPLE: I always see the Abbot in my dreams before he comes to L.A. Last time, I could see my mother and father going to the airport to travel to the United States. I looked inside the airplane and thought it was too small; I wondered how we all could get in. However, when I got inside, I saw the airplane getting bigger. It had many Buddhas inside, as well as Bhikshus and Bhikshunis who had come to ask the Abbot to lecture for them. Also, I wonder why it gets hot after the Abbot leaves, yet every time he comes, it rains the day before?

THE MASTER: Because the heavens don't like me and they don't welcome me! And so, heaven starts crying.

DISCIPLE: After the Abbot left last time, I broke a rule. I ate food that my mother had intended to give to the Buddhas for an offering and I didn't let her know. Then my upper lip broke out with a bad rash. When she asked me what I had done, I didn't tell her. When she found out, she got real mad at me and threw the fruit at me.

THE MASTER: If you're off by a hair's breadth in the beginning, you will miss your goal by a thousand miles. What is cultivation? It is simply getting rid of your faults—— *all* of your faults. The greatest fault of all is affliction. Where does affliction come from? It comes from ignorance. Since you don't understand, you grow afflicted. Afflicted, you are unable to resolve your problems and the more bewildered you are, the more afflictions you have. Afflictions accumulate by the day and by the month until they're piled as high as Mt. Sumeru. How high is Mt. Sumeru? The heaven we can see is called the Heaven of the Four Kings, and this heaven is located only half way up Mt. Sumeru. Mt. Sumeru is twice as high. Our afflictions and karmic obstacles are as high as Mt. Sumeru. They are as large as Mt. Sumeru. So in cultivation, you have to get rid of your afflictions bit by bit. For every bit of affliction you get rid of, you can equally reduce your karmic obstacles. As your karmic obstacles decrease, your wisdom will increase proportionally. Why do we have so little wisdom? Because we have so much affliction. Once we rid ourselves of our afflictions, then our wisdom will naturally manifest. Why is the Buddha called the Enlightened One, the One of Great Wisdom? It's because the Buddha has cut off all affliction. However, it's not that he has cut it off, rather, he has transformed it; turned it into Bodhi. Bodhi is wisdom; it's enlightening to the Way. If everyone possessed this wisdom, they would have no affliction and they wouldn't be stupid. Why do I say that affliction can be turned into Bodhi? It's like ice. Ice is basically water. Ice can turn into water and water can freeze into ice. When the weather warms up, the ice melts into water; when the weather turns cold, the water freezes into ice. If people are happy, they will have wisdom; if they are afflicted, they will be stupid. Stupidity is just affliction. Happiness is just Bodhi. This is just as easy as turning your hand over. The back of your hand is affliction, and the palm of your hand is Bodhi. Just turn your hand over! It's not at all difficult.

As for one of my young disciples--if he has light, he is wise. If he is in darkness, that's stupidity. What is darkness? Stealing food to eat! Knowing that you were wrong and deciding to reform, is having light and wisdom. When you are stealing, you sneak off to a dark place where no one will see you--that is, you have no light. If you had light you wouldn't steal food; you'd be afraid that someone would see you! Although this is a small matter, it is extremely important. So I say, if you're off by a hair in the beginning, you will miss your goal by a thousand miles. If you don't cultivate, no one watches over you and you can pretty much do what you like. But as soon as you decide to cultivate, the Dharma protectors and the gods and dragons of the eight-fold division will take charge of you, and you can't be casual at all.

Someone is thinking, "Dharma Master, I don't believe a word you say. He ate those leechee nuts and they had too much fire in them and so his lip broke out in a rash." Very well, I won't eat any then...to say nothing of stealing them. That takes care of that problem.

* * * * *

*When the butcher puts down his
 knife,
He can immediately become a
 Buddha.*

Butchers kill animals every day. If, one day, a butcher

feels that it is wrong to kill them and puts the knife down, he can become a Buddha on the spot--he too, can certify to the fruit. So don't look at people's faults. If they recognize their faults and wake up, that is a good sign. My little disciple stole the leechees and then realized he was wrong, and so there is hope for him. It's not that important and he shouldn't feel embarassed. If you have made a mistake and everyone knows about it, then they can help you and you won't have these shady problems again. Such a small child recognizing his mistakes is a good sign. In the future, he will be able to cultivate. The important thing is to recognize your mistakes and then change.

KEEP THE PRECEPTS

Today, we will talk about cause and effect. If you plant a good cause, you will reap a good effect; if you plant an evil cause you will reap an evil effect. Therefore, we must be very careful about planting causes. Don't plant unwholesome causes, plant good ones. This is especially important in cultivating the Way, because

*If the cause ground is
not true,
The fruit will be twisted.*

If you do a bad job on the cause ground, there will be many different and complex, detrimental effects. So if one is not careful in beginning, one will be harmed in the end.

In cultivating, we must keep the precepts, be patient, and charitable. Charity means giving valuable things to others, not expecting others to give to you. Wealth must be given; that is an obvious act of giving. But the imperceptible forms of giving must be practiced as well. For example, in not hating others, we give. In not even having a trace of hatred we give it away. That means whether someone is good or bad to you, you do not hate them. That's called giving. Greed should be given away. One should not be greedy. Give greed away. Give it to whom? You say, "I don't want to give it to others, because that would be wrong, wouldn't it?" Then give your greed to empty space. Give your hatred to empty space. Give your stupidity to empty space. Don't be selfish. Don't have the slightest trace of selfishness. In your mind, always be pure and clear.

*When the mind is clear, the moon appears
in the water.
When the will is fixed, the sky has no
clouds.
When the mind is calm, a hundred problems
vanish.
When the will is fixed, all things are
secure.*

All this comes about when the mind is pure.

Keeping precepts means keeping them absolutely. Do not even entertain a single thought of killing. Cut off the causes of killing as well as the conditions of killing. Get rid of the karma of killing and don't indulge in the methods of killing. When these four aspects do not arise, there is no killing.

This also means to not let the causes, conditions, methods, or karma of stealing arise. One then obtains purity. The same holds true for sexual misconduct, taking intoxicants, and false speech. Cutting them off is what counts. You should not receive precepts and then fail to keep them by casually lying and cheating people. Don't do that. If you cheat others, they will cheat you. That is a case of not being true on the cause ground and in the future, your retribution will be miserable indeed. So no matter who you are--a person who has left home or one who is at home, you must strictly observe the precepts. Keep them without ever lying. Think: "I would rather cut off my head than tell a lie. I would rather cut off my head than kill. I would rather cut off my head than create the karma of stealing. I would rather cut off my head than give rise to karma of sexual misconduct. I would rather cut off my head than create karma of lying. I would rather cut off my head than create karma of taking intoxicants.

At all times one must keep the pure precepts. Don't wear a false front to cover your ugly face. Cultivators must be models for people in the world. You cannot be untrue in keeping the precepts. This is very important. Don't leave home and think you can sluff through. If you just want to cruise your way through, why bother to leave home? Lay folks can be a bit more casual about things, but really, they shouldn't be sloppy either.

*One should follow the good
And reform what is evil.*

ON THE GREAT COMPASSION MANTRA...

(Someone asked about the efficacy of reciting the Great Compassion Mantra either silently or out loud. The Master answered):

Silently or out loud, the effect is the same. If you recite out loud, you shouldn't have false thinking but should hold the mantra singlemindedly. Silently, you should do the same. The merit is the same. There is no way to even think about the merit and virtue of the mantra. It's inconceivable. No matter what you need it for, it works. If you constantly hold the mantra, you can cure all of the eighty-four thousand kinds of illnesses. The Medicine Master Mantra is also very effective for illness. There is also another mantra. It is the one spoken by Moonlight Bodhisattva in *The Dharani Sutra*. His vow power can cure everyone's illness, no matter what it is. You need only recite his mantra and you will have a response.

I am not a doctor. Once, in Manchuria, there was a person who got a millipede in his ear, and it bore into his brain. Such a person should certainly have died. There's no way to cure this type of illness unless you operate, and that's terribly dangerous! When millipedes get old they can do mischief and turn into people. However, when I used this mantra on him, he got better. The millipede was removed. And so whatever illness you have, this Bodhisattva is able to treat it. He can miraculously operate on you and heal you. Most people won't believe a state like this, but it's for real.

THE TRICKY GEOMANCIST

Geomancers have confused people in both the United States and in Chung Kuo. In the United States, it's only because the geomancers here have not yet learned to speak English that they haven't been able to get to the English speaking Americans. But now, the geomancers have gotten together with the realtors so that when the realtors go to look at a house, they bring along a geomancer with them. The geomancers have been advertising themselves in the papers a lot. Now it so happened, in the L.A. area, that a real estate agent and a geomancer went to look at a house together with a client. The geomancer brought along a *feng hsui* compass to check out the situation around the house. At one point he asked the client, "What's your birth sign?" The client replied, "The sign of the dragon." The geomancer said, "Oh, this house is just made for you! Quickly! Buy it! If you buy this house you will immediately become rich!" Now in this particular instance this person who was looking to buy the house half believed and half disbelieved in geomancy, and so shortly after, he called in another person to go look at the house with him again. Now maybe, when this geomancer went to see so many houses, he plain lost track of the faces of his prospective clients, and so after awhile, when this client came back again and asked to be shown the same house, the geomancer, having forgotten that he'd already been told, asked the client again what his birth sign was. This time the client replied, "My birth sign is that of the snake." The geomancer said, "Quickly, Buy it! If you buy this house you will get incredibly rich!" Then the person buying the house said, "Didn't you tell me before that this house was especially made for someone with the sign of the dragon!" The geomancer darted his eyes about nervously and said, "Well, uh, dragons and snakes are in the same family--what's the difference! They're relatives."

Now, take a look at this situation. That's really trying to talk one's way out of a situation by saying that snakes and dragons are of the same family. Because of this incident, the person in mention couldn't believe in geomancy anymore. So no matter what others may do, we here at the City of Ten Thousand Buddhas must never speak falsely. Don't try to cheat people. All the crook geomancers are getting together with the realty agents; the realty agents are introducing their clients to the geomancers. This type of partnership causes the businesses of both parties to flourish. The realtors give the geomancers a commission for getting people to buy their houses, and the geomancers can make money off of real estate without ever getting a license. So things in this world are getting really weird. When I heard this story, I felt that it was something to learn from, so I am telling you about this now.

AT THE CITY OF TEN THOUSAND BUDDHAS
WE SHOULD CULTIVATE THE WAY

This place, the City of Ten Thousand Buddhas, has really fresh air. It's a really good place to cultivate the Way. Being able to encounter such a good place in which to cultivate, if one still doesn't cultivate, then one is really wasting one's time in vain. It isn't easy to find such a place in the entire world where people are cultivating the Way and following the rules. But it all depends on whether you *want* to cultivate the Way or not. No one is going to force you. No matter how much you want to apply your effort, this place can accommodate your practice. So the line to match tonight is "AT THE CITY OF TEN THOUSAND BUDDHAS, WE SHOULD CULTIVATE THE WAY." You should cultivate well and not let the time go by emptily.

EARTH STORE BODHISATTVA

You could say that Earth Store Bodhisattva is the most dumb of Bodhisattvas and also the most intelligent. Why dumb? Because he does the things that no one else wants to do. He can bear what others can't bear and yield what others can't yield. When his parents were really mean to him, it didn't make any difference, he was filial just the same. That's why within Buddhism, Earth Store Bodhisattva is known as the Bodhisattva of great filiality and also the Bodhisattva of great vows. He said, "Until the hells are empty, I will never become a Buddha." Until every single living being is taken across, he doesn't want to attain proper and equal enlightenment. Just take a look at this kind of vow-power-- doesn't it seem kind of dumb? On the other hand, we can also say he is the most intelligent Bodhisattva. That's because he stands out above everyone else. He transcends all his peers. Someone asks, "Well, is he trying to be special?" No. He does what others don't want to do and aren't able to do, and so we can say that he is the most intelligent Bodhisattva. In short, it can be said of Earth Store Bodhisattva that he has great vows, great conduct, great wisdom, and great compassion.

In Chung Kuo there are four holy mountains: Wu T'ai Mountain is the Bodhimanda of Manjushri Bodhisattva; P'u T'ou is the Bodhimanda of Kuan Yin Bodhisattva; Mei Shan is the Bodhimanda of Universal Worthy Bodhisattva; and Chiu Hua Mountain is the sacred Way Place devoted to Earth Store Bodhisattva. Earth Store Bodhisattva embodies the vow-power of all Bodhisattvas, the conduct of all Bodhisattvas, the wisdom of all Bodhisattvas, and the compassion of all Bodhisattvas. His power of vows is truly inconceivable, and so is his wisdom as well as his accomplishment.

Those of us who are living in the Dharma Ending Age should definitely recite the name of Earth Store Bodhisattva more and make vows like this Bodhisattva. In this way we can help the world avoid horrendous disasters. From times long ago until today the world has never been in such great danger. Why? Do you really need to ask? It's because every country is in the nuclear race, intent on making weapons which are designed to totally eliminate mankind. The most treacherous thing now is the laser. In Chung Wen it is called the "death ray." With this death ray, everyone is going to be destroyed, leaving no one to survive. We are going to exterminate all of humanity. Exterminate! Exterminate! This death ray has appeared in the world as a warning, telling people, "Don't continue to do evil things. If you continue to do bad things, all of humanity will be exterminated. The sea of suffering is boundless. Quickly Turn around and you will reach the other shore. You should practice filiality, fraternity, loyalty, integrity, propriety, righteousness, incorruptibility, and a sense of shame. You should embody those eight virtues, and then humanity will not be exterminated. Otherwise, we have invented a weapon called the death ray and it is designed to annihilate mankind."

Not only will this weapon exterminate all of humanity, but all those in the animal realm as well. Every living thing will be exterminated. And once everything is exterminated, the world will turn into emptiness. There will be no more people, no more material world, no creatures--what will be left? Emptiness. The world will go back to the source. So, how can you in this day and age, still be hung up on getting rich, getting some official position, seeking fame, seeking profit? You try to get a reputation at any cost and in the process you hurt a lot of people. That's really being stupid! People like this don't even recognize what day and what age they are living in. So stop and think. We have these few decades in which to live and during that time, if we don't amass some merit and virtue, then we will have lived our lives in vain.

Some of you have come especially today to bow to the Ten Thousand Buddhas at the City of Ten Thousand Buddhas, but it's really important that you truly bring forth the Bodhi mind. You should see that there's nothing so extraordinary or desirable about anything in this world. No matter how wealthy you become, even if you have all the gold, silver, and diamonds in this world, when the time comes for you to die, what of it can you take with you? You can't take any gold, you can't take any silver, nor can you take any diamonds--you die emptihanded. If you wait until you die to be left emptihanded, it's not as good as taking advantage of your lifetime to do useful things with your wealth and thereby amass merit and virtue. If you put your wealth to good use, then your life would not be a total waste. Since the Buddhas and Bodhisattvas are helping you so that everything about your life is compliant and easy, you should certainly want to repay their kindness.

You should wake up from your dream. Quickly bring forth the resolve for Bodhi. Don't wait until you are old to cultivate the Way. The lonely graves are mostly filled with those who died young. And remember that an inch of time is a moment of life; and an inch of time is worth an inch of gold. If you lose the gold it's possible to get it back, but if you lose an inch of life, it's impossible to regain it.

Smart people don't do muddled things; muddled people don't ever think to do smart things. And so the good get together and the bad gather in gangs. People gravitate to their own kind. Now you are here to witness the very beginning of the City of Ten Thousand Buddhas. For instance, on the two sides of this main hall there are subsidiary halls. On one side is the Hall of Merit and Virtue and on the other is the Hall of Rebirth. In the Hall of Merit and Virtue and the Hall of Long Life, those who have helped to establish the City of Ten Thousand Buddhas will be remembered in the future. And in the Hall of Rebirth, you can place the ashes of your ancestors or set up a memorial plaque for them in commemoration. That is a filial act. With those rebirth plaques, people can establish merit and virtue.

The City of Ten Thousand Buddhas is in its beginning stages. In 1976 I acquired the City of Ten Thousand Buddhas and at that time everyone looked on from the side lines and figured I must be kidding. They just stood on and watched. No one offered to help. They all said, "That's a huge place and he's such a poor monk. It's for sure he will lose it within a year. He will have to close the doors and declare bankruptcy." No one resolved to help. But the doors didn't close in a year. It has been almost seven years now. It could be said that in these seven years the City has prospered more and more each year. Why wasn't I afraid? Because I am not selfish and I'm not out for self-benefit. Whatever I do, I do on behalf of all of Buddhism. I never calculate in terms of myself alone. And because of that, everyday there are more people who leave the homelife and more Sutras are being translated into English. And now the Ten Thousand Buddhas have come and they are glowing and shining their light on the City of Ten Thousand Buddhas. These seven years have passed in a blink of an eye and I still say we are at the beginning stages of our development. Earlier I showed you our new dining hall, which is being constructed. Both sides of the building will seat 2,000 people. Not only that, but we are beginning to build "the Great Hall." The Great Hall will seat 10,000. Ten Thousand will be able to come and bow to the Buddha. We can certainly say that in all of America, there's no Way Place that can hold so many people who can bow to the Buddha all at once. In fact, in all of

Asia as well, you won't find such a big hall. You ask, "Why do you want such a big place, anyway?" I'll tell you. Even that hall can't be considered too big. America is an international country. All races and nationalities come to America. In such a country, a small Way-place won't be big enough to hold all those who want to come and worship. So as an international Way-place within Buddhism, if we don't have a hall that can hold ten thousand people, then we are not functioning on an appropriately large scale.

ON TOP OF WONDERFUL ENLIGHTENMENT MOUNTAIN, THE BUDDHA NODS HIS HEAD AND SMILES

Wonderful Enlightenment Mountain is our mountain here and on top of that mountain the Buddha nods his head and smiles. All the Buddhas of the ten directions nod and smile. "The Buddha smiles" has many meanings. The most important meaning it has is that we people are so upside-down and yet we don't cultivate. When will the time come for us to bring forth the great Bodhi mind? That's what the Buddhas are expressing with their smiles. It's the smile of a mother thinking about her son's returning home. "When will he be able to come back?" That's another meaning behind the smile. The smile also represents the Buddhas' delight at the cultivators in the City of Ten Thousand Buddhas who practice the Way and bring forth the resolve for Bodhi and work hard to seek after the unsurpassed Way. These Buddhas are rejoicing. On the other hand, the Buddhas also see that some of us here are always doing stupid things. No matter how you exhort them to change their faults and renew themselves, they don't change and they continue in the same old way. That is another meaning behind the Buddhas' smiles. The Buddhas witness living beings in the world who are unable to renounce greed, anger, and stupidity, and they find this really pitiful, and so the Buddhas are there nodding and smiling.

Also, the Buddhas see that there are living beings who very, very clearly know that the Proper Dharma is the right thing to practice, yet they don't cultivate the Proper Dharma but still maintain deviant knowledge and deviant views. That's another meaning behind the Buddhas' nods and smiles. So everyone should think about this and try to match this line.

IF YOU DON'T SEEK THE GREAT WAY,
YOU AREN'T A GREAT HERO

*If one doesn't seek the Great Way and get off the
   confused path,
One will fall short of being a great hero, even if
   one has a lot of talent.
A hundred years are like a spark struck from a
   piece of flint.
An entire lifetime is like a bubble floating on
   the water.
Put down this wealth. It doesn't really belong
   to one.
But one's offense karma follows right after one.
It's hard to cheat oneself.
One's gold and silver might be piled high as a
   mountain,
But could one possibly use it to buy off the
   Ghost of Impermanence?*

   This poem, by a writer of old, says that human life is impermanent, occupations are impermanent, and worldly pleasures are the cause of pain. All the happiness of the world contains suffering. If you want to get out of suffering and attain bliss, you should cultivate the Way. In cultivation you must first get rid of faults and understand how to regulate yourself and return to propriety. You must get rid of desire and cut off love. Once you understand these matters, then you can cultivate the Way. People are born because of desire for sex and die because of desire for sex. This is "going along with the flow" and getting born. By going against the flow, one can accomplish Sagehood. To "oppose the flow" is to turn away from what is worldly. You don't love what worldly people love. You are not confused by what worldly people are confused by. You are not greedy for what worldly people are greedy for. Those who go along with the flow lose their sense of direction, so that the farther they go, the more lost they get. They are basically on the wrong road.
   So don't fail to seek the Way. If you want to get out of birth and death, you have to seek the Way. To seek the Way you need a true Bright-Eyed Wise Advisor who understands how to teach you to cultivate the Way and who can cause you to end death and enable you to stop the cycle of rebirth.
   If one doesn't seek the Great Way and get off the confused path,/ One will fall short of being a great hero, even if one has a lot of talent. If you don't seek the Way, you are wasting your talents. You put them to use in

vain. Would a Great Hero do that? No. In fact, that's a really pathetic way to live your life. All people have the wisdom and virtuous conduct of the Thus Come One, but if they don't cultivate, they can't realize it.

A hundred years are like a spark struck from a piece of flint. No matter how long the lifespan, it's just a flash in the pan. It really isn't much. A hundred years go by in the blink of an eye, the space of a breath. It's really nothing special at all. *An entire lifetime is like a bubble floating on the water.* This body is like a bit of foam on the sea--empty and false. It's nothing real that should keep you hanging around. Nothing worth lingering on for.

Put down this wealth, it doesn't really belong to one. When the time comes to die, your own spouse won't stand in for you. Your money can't take your place. You have to put it all down at that time. It's not yours anymore. "I leave descendants," you argue. But they are not you and don't even really have much connection with you.

But one's offense karma follows right after one. The karma of killing, the karma of stealing, the karma of sexual misconduct, the karma of lying and the karma of taking intoxicants follows you when you die. You can't cheat yourself. You created it and you have to undergo it. *It's hard to cheat yourself./ One's gold and silver might be piled high as a mountain,*/Some people really do amass that kind of wealth--gold, antiques, jade. *But could one possibly use it to buy off the Ghost of Impermanence?* Can you buy off the Ghost of Impermanence? If you leave home and don't really cultivate--what are you waiting for? Leaving home is not a matter of eating confusedly and waiting for death--letting the time pass in vain.

You should be truly diligent. If you're off by a bit in the beginning, you'll be off by a thousand miles in the end. You can't be the least bit careless.

Without even dismounting,
The generals gallop off into a distance.

Advance and go forward with diligence!

PATIENCE

In cultivation, if one is off by just a tiny bit, one won't succeed. Because one is off by just that tiny bit, the further one runs, the further off one gets. In the beginning we have no false thinking. Then we give rise to false thinking and,

Off by a hair in the beginning,
We miss our goal by a thousand miles.

That little bit of false thinking covers up the true. If one gets rid of that little bit, then the true will manifest. When the true manifests, it is like the sky: cloudless for ten thousand miles; there is nothing at all in it. Without anything, all attachments are broken. Without attachments, one is not attached to good states or to evil states. One is not attached to having states or to not having them. That's how we speak about it' but *doing* it is really hard. No-attachment itself is liberation. If you attain liberation, there are no more problems. But it's not easy to be liberated. If you have even a hair's breadth of attachment, you can't be liberated.

If one is to get rid of attachments, where does one start? You start from enduring the unendurable: yielding where you cannot yield, eating what can't be eaten, and taking what you cannot take. It's said, "A ten-thousand story building starts from the ground up." You have to start from the basics. Then, bit by bit, you will get rid of your ignorance and afflictions. Cultivation is just like polishing a mirror which is covered with dust. You rub it clean and then it reflects light. However, it's easy to say, and hard to do. From the ten directions things happen that are hard to recognize. Not recognizing them, you are turned by them. If you recognize the state, you can turn the state. In order to be able to turn the state you must employ the paramita of patience and be able to bear all situations. There must be nothing you cannot endure. If you can't bear it, then you won't get through the "gate." You will be stuck. If you can bear it, and not be nervous, you will get through the "gate." So in cultivation, the most important thing is patience. Patience is just giving. Patience is morality. It is also vigor, Ch'an samadhi, and wisdom. Without wisdom, you won't have patience. Without Ch'an samadhi, you won't be patient. Without vigor, you won't have the energy to be patient--you won't have the patience to bear up under vigor. Also, you must bear up under holding the precepts. It's hard to keep precepts, but you should bear up under it and do no evil but offer up all good. Being patient is just giving. What are you giving away? Your afflictions. That's what we say. But when the time comes to do it, it's really very hard. Even though it's hard we still have to do it. If we don't do it because it's hard, then we won't be able to cultivate and will never accomplish our fruit of the Way.

So patience is great. If you can master it, you can get to the other shore. Without it, you won't get to the other shore. You could call patience a boat. You ride the boat of patience in order to reach the other shore of vigor.

For example, when lecturing, don't be nervous, but don't fall asleep either. If you sweat when you have to lecture but then feel comfortable when you're asleep...well...that's not having patience. You should start from when you're small and practice patience until you have no "self." If you sweat now from nervousness when asked to lecture, what will you be like in the future? If the Emperor bowed to you, you would be worse off. So you listen and listen, but it's of no use. You must go *do* it. Whoever can be patient will gain great blessings and wisdom, and great happiness. So cultivate patience.

You all think that I have no patience, but I have the most patience. See? All day long I get bullied by my disciples. They all know that I am easily bullied and so they do so at their will. Even my young disciples bully me. When the time comes for one of them to lecture, he shakes his head "no." He knows if he doesn't lecture, he won't get punished, so he doesn't listen. See? A lot of people imitate you. They think, "You are supposed to be a teacher but you can't even manage your young disciples. What kind of teacher are you? Shameless!" They scold me.

HELP OTHER WAY PLACES

Buddhism has just started to spread in the West in the last few decades. Whenever a Buddhist Way-place is being established, it is very difficult for those involved, so no one should be unwilling to help anyone else, each one fighting for himself--I being jealous of you and you being jealous of me. That's the way everyone has been, and so it hasn't been easy to spread Buddhism. Now everyone at Gold Mt. Monastery, Gold Wheel Temple, and the City of Ten Thousand Buddhas should expand the measure of their minds. The measure of our minds should be so vast that it exhausts empty space and pervades the Dharma Realm. If someone else's Way-place doesn't exist, then one's own Way-place doesn't exist. Wherever there is a Buddhist Way-place, we should protect it and aid it. Nor should we discriminate and say, "This Way-place is one with which I have certain emotional ties, so I'll protect it, but I don't have such ties with that Way-place, so I won't protect it." We should not make emotional ties our criterion. We should make Buddhism our criterion. The establishment of any Buddhist Way-place of proper Dharma is another step for the greater glory of Buddhism. Therefore, we must expand the measure of our minds. Even if people are jealous of us, we won't be jealous of them, and it's not for certain people are actually jealous of us. Due to this consideration, if we are able to take Buddhism as the criterion in our actions, then whoever is nurturing Buddhism and spreading it far and wide should receive our assistance.

DON'T CHEAT YOURSELF

(Several Buddhist songs were sung and then the Abbot began:)

Music is one of the Six Arts, which are:

1. Propriety
2. Music
3. Archery
4. Charioteering
5. Writing
6. Computation

1. "Propriety" refers to the *Book of Rites*, in which

people are told what their duties are and the right way to act for every occasion. For example, when you see an Emperor, you should kneel and bow, and there are appropriate manners for greeting a President or high official. When you see your parents you should be very respectful. Children should sit in the corner of the room.

2. "Music" is used to cheer people up. Sometimes people get very depressed, but when they hear appropriate music, they become happy. Sometimes the joy music brings can even lead to tears.

3. "Archery" is an ancient art which requires mindfulness and agility.

4. "Charioteering" referred of old to skill in driving horse-drawn vehicles. Nowadays it would refer to driving cars in general. It is also considered an art.

5. "Writing" refers to calligraphy.

6. "Computation" means counting numbers: 1, 10, 100, 1,000, 10,000, and so forth. There are so many numbers that one could never count to their end. Even computers can't count to the end of numbers. By adding a zero to the number one, you have 10; add another zero and you have 100; keep adding zeros and you get 1,000, 10,000, and on and on. Who knows how many zeros there could be? Who could keep track? You could fill empty space and the Dharma Realm with zeros and what would the total be? You can't get at the total because there's no end to numbers. Even if you filled space and the Dharma Realm with zeros, you could still add one more and one more. The whole thing starts with the number one. If it weren't for that number, then the zeros wouldn't amount to anything. But although numbers are endless, we should understand them in their limited aspect. Therefore, people study computation as one of the Six Arts.

Confucius had some three thousand students, but only seventy-two of them understood deeply the Six Arts in their entirety.

Music is one of the Six Arts and singing has its place, too, in Buddhism. If you sing, perhaps you will make people so happy that they get enlightened, it's not for sure. You might dispel their afflictions to the point that they are so happy--ahah!--they get enlightened. It's possible. There are all kinds of expedient Dharma doors, and music is one of them. However, as you study more Buddhist doctrine, you will naturally set aside more and more worldly knowledge. For every part of Buddhist doctrine you pick up, you will put down just that much worldly doctrine. If one side is heavy, the other side is light. It's like a scale. If you understand more Buddhism, you will be less

burdened with worldly concerns.
Everyone should study the doctrines of Buddhism; listen to the Sutras and Dharma. However, people should understand this for sure: you should actually do as much as you know. Don't just learn it and fail to do it, like the disciple who told us that she knew the blanket would keep her warm, but she didn't use it. She insisted on fighting with the cold and getting angry at it to see who would lose out. She made a good analogy out of it. She said that knowing very clearly the Buddhadharma could make her free, but not using it, is just like knowing the blanket would keep off the cold but ignoring it. She's very intelligent.
When you study the Buddhadharma, you should learn to always know your own faults. Don't just give yourself high hats and gold leaf your own face saying, "Do you see me? I'm the greatest. Don't you know I'm number one in this and that? Do you know how intelligent I am? I never make mistakes. I do everything well. I don't do anything poorly." Such a Buddhist disciple will quickly wither away and fall by the wayside. Such a person won't be able to truly advance in the Way. Why not? Because such a one thinks that he or she is already so good that there's no way for them to make any progress. To be like this is just like saying one has become a Buddha when one has not yet done so. This is like a certain self-styled "guru" who bragged, saying, "Don't you know? This Dharma Master is enlightened. He's incredible! And I'm just like him! Look at that. We're just alike. We're the same in cultivation, brothers, with the same wisdom. I know what he knows; I can do what he can do."
There are others who claim to be enlightened and can even state the time and place it happened. "When I was eating, I got enlightened. I ate lunch and then wasn't hungry. That was my enlightenment." Or, "I got enlightened wearing clothes, knowing I wouldn't be cold." A few years ago, an "enlightened patriarch" came to the Buddhist Lecture Hall in San Francisco to debate with me. He said he was the same as the Sixth Patriarch; that he got enlightened just the way the Sixth Patriarch did. I said, "That's great. You know, after the Sixth Patriarch was enlightened, there was a Korean named Chin Ta-pei who wanted to remove his head and take it back to Korea to make offerings to it. You haven't died and that's great. I'll take your head right now!" I scared him so much he stood up and ran. I said, "Why are you running?"
He said, "Even Shakyamuni Buddha would be afraid to have his head cut off!"
I said, "How do you know he would have been afraid to

have someone cut off his head?"

He said, "Well, no one cut off his head."

I said, "That doesn't prove he would have been afraid of having his head cut off."

But we didn't even finish our conversation before he ran off. He said he wanted to study with me but then he introduced himself as enlightened, so there was obviously nothing left for him to study. So he sent a relative to the Way-place to steal the Buddhadharma. She didn't say who she was, but I knew the minute I saw her. I said, "Everyone be careful. There's a mouse here who's come to steal the Buddhadharma." In fact, she did look like a mouse. She probably was a mouse turned into a person. Her features were mousy enough. She studied for awhile and then left. She had left a sixty dollar rent deposit which she didn't take in her hurry to be gone. But five or six years later she came back for the money so I gave it to her. I said, "I don't sell the Buddhadharma here. You'd be better off to take the money back." So people who study the Buddhadharma must always know their errors. My verse is very important and you should all remember it. It says,

> *Truly recognize your own faults,*
> *Don't discuss the faults of others.*
> *Others' faults are just my own:*
> *Being of one substance with everyone is called Great Compassion.*

That's how you should be. Students of the Buddhadharma shouldn't think that they are number one. They shouldn't think, "Do you see me? I'm a great Dharma protector." That's upside down. Or, "I understand the Buddhadharma." If you really understand it, you wouldn't say such things. People who understand Buddhadharma don't praise themselves. People who say they are good have problems inside. Buddhists must not praise themselves and deprecate others, or speak of other's faults. So when you lecture, if you can speak about your own faults and how you are wrong, you are a real student of Buddhism. But, if you still have the idea that you are "number one" in your mind, or the thought that you really cultivate, then that's too bad. Don't be proud. Pride incurs harm; humility brings benefit. This is especially true for cultivators: they should be models. If you still can't understand real principle and cheat yourself, no matter how long you cheat yourself, you'll never end birth and death.

THE ETERNAL BUDDHANATURE

At the very start, before heaven and earth came into being, there weren't any people. There was no earth, no living beings, nor anything called a world. Basically, none of these things existed at all. And then, at the onset of the kalpa when things were coming into being, people gradually came to exist. Ultimately, where do they come from? Some say that people evolved from monkeys. But what do the monkeys evolve from? If people evolved from monkeys, then why are there no people evolving from monkeys right now? This is really strange. People who propagate this kind of theory basically don't have any understanding. They are just trying to set up some special theory. So there's the theory of evolution which says that people came from monkeys. Why couldn't it be the case that people evolved from mice? Or caterpillars? Why couldn't we say that mice evolved from people or caterpillars evolved from people? In general, there can be said to be four kinds of beings--flying, swimming, walking, and plants. Those with blood and breath are called animals, and the plants refers to all kinds of grasses and trees and flowers. Where do all of those four kinds of beings come from? What is their origin? Their origin is the Buddhanature. If there was no Buddhanature, everything would be annihilated. The Buddhanature is the only thing that passes through ten thousand generations and all time without being destroyed. From the Buddhanature comes Bodhisattvas, Sound Hearers, Those Enlightened to Conditions, gods, asuras, people, animals, ghosts, and hell beings. Those are the beings of the Ten Dharma Realms, and the Ten Dharma Realms are not apart from a single thought of the mind. This single thought of the mind is just the seed of the Buddhanature. It's just another name for the Buddhanature--the one true thought.

So, people are transformed from the Buddhas and animals are those who have fallen from the realm of humans. This is all explained very clearly in the *Ten Dharma Realms*. Stupid people say that the origin of humans is the monkey and there are others who say that people came from pigs. For example, some cultures still worship animal gods. People in India say that the cow is a divine spirit. And those are just views that are off the mark--one-sided views. They are a result of only knowing a little bit and not understanding the complete picture. With such ideas, the world catapults in confusion and chaos. People who believe in such things write books and set up theories, they categorize everything to fit into their theories, claiming this to be this and that to be that. So we have science and philosophy--everything is put in its own little niche. But ultimately, what's this all about? It's a case of not having anything to do and looking for something to do. People like that are not able to simply sit around, so after they eat their fill, they go about setting up their own theories to confuse people by. This is why most people are so perplexed.

Ultimately, where did humans come from? How did they come about? In investigating this question, we might consider how chickens came about. Which came first, the chicken or the egg? If you don't have a chicken, then there's no way you can have an egg, and if you don't have an egg, how can a chicken hatch? So this problem has no solution. As far as people are concerned, were there women first, or were there men first? If you claim that the men came first, how do you explain that men are born from women? And, without women, how can there be any men? If you claim that the women were first to appear, how can you explain that both men and women are required to produce more people? Without a man, how can another woman be conceived? In investigating this question, it is impossible to come up with a clear solution. This is because all of this began so very long ago, we've all forgotten.

Ultimately, what's the answer? Well, ultimately, everything comes from the Buddhanature. Everything comes into being naturally: from nothing something manifests and that something transforms once more into nothing. This happens without end, over and over again; an infinite on-going series of production and transformation.

For example, the bugs that appear in the dry rice: basically, the rice just sits there in the bag without any worms, but suddenly they appear. You may ask how they come about, if originally there weren't any worms. Rice is not sentient, it's not alive, so how is it the case that it can produce bugs since bugs are creatures with feeling? Here is a case of something devoid of feeling producing something that has feeling. Investigate this problem to its ultimate point. Consider how it will be when heaven and earth are destroyed by the "death ray" (laser), to the point that the world and all of humanity are completely annihilated. There will still be the spiritual souls of those living beings who once dwelled in the world. The Buddhanature will continue to exist. And it is the Buddhanature that can make things appear from nothing, for it can create mankind and all living beings. And so, even if you insist this is not the case and say, "It's certain that people evolved from monkeys," your theory just won't stand.

Take a look at Americans. They have their own habit patterns. And so do the people of Russia. And the same goes for the French, English, and so on. "But," you say, "In America, there are all kinds of people." Yes, that's true, they branch out into many sub-cultures. Since there are so many kinds of people, how can you say that mankind evolved from only one particular kind of creature? The people of each and every country have a generally different appearance. There are yellow people, white people, black people, red people, and brown people. Where did the black people come from? Where did the white people come from? Where did the yellow people originate from and where did the red people and the brown people come from? If you discuss this back and forth you won't be able to pin-point a particular origin. But you can explain it all by returning it to the Buddhanature: from nothing comes something and something returns to nothing. The transformations continue endlessly, over and over again. This is the source behind it all.

Now this is a theory that can hold up. But although this theory is one that holds true, very few people have the wisdom to reach an understanding of it. People are transformed from nothing; we manifest from out of nothing. That is the nature of all living beings. They appear from nothing. Originally, living beings did not exist, but then they came about through transformation. In cultivating the Way, we want to get back to the place where from something we become nothing. This is called "going back to the origin and returning to the source"--returning to the original Buddhanature. "What good is there to this?" you ask. Well, what good is there in being a person? If you return to the original nature you can quickly accomplish the Buddha Way. Even if heaven and earth were to no longer exist, the Buddhanature would still be ever-present. And even if all of mankind were finished off by the "death ray," the Buddhanature would still abide, be forever indestructible.

Why did I bring this up tonight? Today is Earth Store Bodhisattva's birthday and his vow power has spurred me on to speak a bit of true principle for all of you. So don't think that everything I say is very ordinary. Don't think that what I tell you is commonplace, because I am outlining the basic principles that explain what people and living beings are all about. This is the principle of transforming something from nothing, and transforming back to nothing again. If you don't believe this, how can you explain that bugs can grow from rice? You may say, "Well, there are certain causes and conditions that bring this about." People in this world are just like those bugs, except that our attachments are stronger and our magical nature is greater. But we cannot begin to compare ourselves with the Buddha. We are just as far from being Buddhas as those bugs are from being people. Compared to the Buddha, we are just like those bugs. When people look at those bugs which grow from the rice we think of them as being really pitiful, that they don't have any purpose in life. Well, the Buddha sees us as just as pitiful. We see that these bugs go through life without knowing anything; they are born unaware of anything and then they die. This principle holds true for us as well. You should all look into this. It's really quite interesting. If you understand this principle, then you can cultivate the Way. So in your cultivation, every day you should be very level and balanced in everything you do.

What does it mean to be balanced? For instance, when you read in the Sutras that "afflictions are just Bodhi and birth and death are just Nirvana," you may find it easy to understand this principle and think this is an easy thing to do. But you can't actually realize this truth. For example, when you read that afflictions are just Bodhi, you think, "afflictions are just Bodhi and since I have afflictions, that's just Bodhi; if I didn't have any afflictions then I wouldn't have any Bodhi." This is not what is meant here. You must change those afflictions and then they will become Bodhi. When you have afflictions, if you can recognize them, then you won't have any afflictions anymore. That's Bodhi. It's not that you put down your afflictions and look for something else that is Bodhi. If you don't have any afflictions, then basically there is nothing whatsoever, so where can the dust alight? When riding on a donkey, don't go looking for the donkey. You need to be balanced. You need to remain level and quiescent at all times so that you don't stir up the slightest wave in your self-nature, and this is the state where afflictions are just Bodhi and birth and death are just Nirvana. If you aren't worried about birth and death and don't see them as a problem, if you feel that if you live you live and if you die you die, that if there's food to eat you eat, and if there's clothes to wear you wear them, and otherwise, it doesn't matter whether or not you eat or wear clothes--if you are not attached to any of this--that is the state of birth and death just being Nirvana. So don't be so attached and drag around those fetters and chains on your body. What fetters and chains? All your bad habits and faults.

Those are your fetters. If you hold on to those fetters, you can't lift up your legs and you can't get to the other shore. The words I am speaking now are very simple, but the meaning is very profound. Don't think that you are so clever and think, "I understand everything that you are saying." If you really understand it all then I can speak Buddhadharma to you and we can investigate how to cultivate the Way. But only if you truly understand. If you don't truly understand, then you still have problems with regard to fame and benefit. You still can't put them down. You can't put down name and you can't put down gain. You see everything as being too important, so how can I talk to you about true Buddhadharma? How can I investigate with you the cultivation of the Way? You should all wake up from your dream! Wake up from your dream!

THE BUDDHIST TEXT TRANSLATION SOCIETY

CHAIRPERSON: The Venerable Tripitaka Master Hsüan Hua
-Abbot of Gold Mountain Monastery, Gold Wheel Monastery, and Tathagata Monastery
-Chancellor of Dharma Realm Buddhist University
-Professor of the Tripitaka and the Dhyanas

PRIMARY TRANSLATION COMMITTEE:

Chairpersons: Venerable Tripitaka Master Hsüan Hua
               Bhikshuni Heng Ch'ih

Members:

Bhikshu Heng Sure
Bhikshu Heng Kuan
Bhikshu Heng Shun
Bhikshu Heng Ch'au
Bhikshu Heng Tso
Bhikshu Heng Ch'i
Bhikshu Heng Gung
Bhikshu Heng Wu
Bhikshu Heng Jau
Bhikshu Heng Ch'ang

Bhikshuni Heng Ch'ing
Bhikshuni Heng Chü
Bhikshuni Heng Chai
Bhikshuni Heng Wen

Bhikshuni Heng Tao
Bhikshuni Heng Ming
Bhikshuni Heng Hsien
Bhikshuni Heng Jieh
Bhikshuni Heng Tsai
Bhikshuni Heng Duan
Bhikshuni Heng Bin
Bhikshuni Heng Liang
Bhikshuni Heng Lyan
Bhikshuni Heng Chia
Upasika Terri Nicholson
Upasaka David Rounds
Upasaka R.B. Epstein
Upasaka Chou Li-jen

REVIEWING COMMITTEE:

Chairpersons: Bhikshu Heng Tso
               Upasaka Kuo Jung Epstein

Members:

Bhikshu Heng Sure
Bhikshu Heng Kuan
Bhikshu Heng Gung
Bhikshu Heng Wu
Bhikshuni Heng Ch'ih
Bhikshuni Heng Chai
Bhikshuni Heng Wen
Bhikshuni Heng Tao

Bhikshuni Heng Hsien
Bhikshuni Heng Tsai
Bhikshuni Heng Duan
Bhikshuni Heng Bin
Bhikshuni Heng Liang
Upasika Hsien Ping-ying
Upasaka David Rounds
Upasaka Chou Li-jen

EDITING COMMITTEE:

Chairperson: Upasika Susan Rounds

Advisor: Bhikshu Heng Kuan

Members:

Bhikshu Heng Sure	Bhikshuni Heng Jieh
Bhikshu Heng Lai	Bhikshuni Heng Tsai
Bhikshu Heng Shun	Bhikshuni Heng Duan
Bhikshu Heng Ch'au	Bhikshuni Heng Bin
Bhikshu Heng Tso	Bhikshuni Heng Liang
Bhikshu Heng Ch'i	Bhikshuni Heng Lyan
Bhikshu Heng Wu	Bhikshuni Heng Chia
Bhikshun Heng Jau	Upasaka R.B. Epstein
Bhikshuni Heng Ch'ih	Upasaka David Rounds
Bhikshuni Heng Ch'ing	Upasika Nancy Lethcoe
Bhikshuni Heng Chü	Upasika Terri Nicholson
Bhikshuni Heng Chai	Upasaka Chou Li-jen
Bhikshuni Heng Wen	Upasika Phuong Kuo Wu
Bhikshuni Heng Tao	Upasika Janet Vickers
Bhikshuni Heng Ming	Upasaka Douglas Powers
Bhikshuni Heng Hsien	Upasika Marion Robertson
	Upasika Marla Wong

CERTIFYING COMMITTEE:

Chairperson: Venerable Tripitaka Master Hsüan Hua

Members:

Bhikshu Heng Sure	Bhikshuni Heng Tao
Bhikshu Heng Kuan	Bhikshuni Heng Hsien
Bhikshu Heng Tso	Upasaka Wong Kuo Chün
Bhikshuni Heng Ch'ih	Upasika Terri Nicholson
Bhikshuni Heng Ch'ing	Upasaka R.B. Epstein
Bhikshuni Heng Wen	Upasika Janet Vickers

CHINESE PUBLICATIONS COMMITTEE:

Chairperson: Upasaka Chou Li-jen

Members:

Bhikshuni Heng Lyan	Bina Teng
Upasika Phuong Kuo Wu	Wong Kuo Ch'ang
Upasika Yao-sen Epstein	

PUBLICATIONS OF THE BUDDHIST TEXT TRANSLATION SOCIETY

All translation works by the Buddhist Text Translation Society are accompanied by extensive interlinear commentaries by the Venerable Tripitaka Master Hsuan Hua, and are available in softcover only, unless otherwise noted.

BUDDHIST SUTRAS

Amitabha Sutra--*This Sutra, which was spoken by the Buddha without being formally requested as in other Sutras, explains the causes and circumstances for rebirth in the Land of Ultimate Bliss of Amitabha (Limitless Light) Buddha. The commentary includes extensive information on common Buddhist terminology, and stories on many of the Buddha's foremost disciples. ISBN 0-917512-01-4, 204 pgs. $8.00.* (Also available in Spanish, *$8.00)*

Brahma Net Sutra- 梵網經講錄 *The Buddha explains the Ten Major and Forty-eight Minor Precepts of the Bodhisattva. Bi-lingual ed., English/Chinese, Vol. 1: ISBN 0-917512-79-0, 300 pgs.; Vol. 2: ISBN 0-917512-88-X, 210 pgs. Two volume set, $18.00. Commentary by the late Venerable Master Hui Seng. Single volume with entire English text, no commentary, is also available. ISBN 0-917512-56-1, 70 pgs. $5.00.*

Dharani Sutra- *Past causes and conditions of the Bodhisattva of Great Compassion, Avalokiteshvara (Kuan Yin), and the various ways to practice the Great Compassion Mantra. A fundamental Secret School method. Second half of volume divided into three sections: first, a line-by-line explanation of the mantra; second, Chinese verses and brush drawings of the division bodies of Kuan Yin corresponding to each of the 84 lines of the mantra; last, drawings and verses in English for each of the 42 Hands and Eyes of Kuan Yin. First English translation. ISBN 0-917512-13-8, 352 pgs., $12.00.*

Dharma Flower (Lotus) Sutra- *Spoken in the last period of his teaching, the Buddha proclaims the ultimate principles of the Dharma, which unites all previous teachings into one. Entire Sutra will be from 15 to 20 volumes when completed. Following volumes have been published to date:*

Volume I, *Introductory Section. ISBN 0-017512-16-2, 85 pgs., $3.95.*
Volume II, Introduction, *Chapter One. ISBN 0-917-512-22-1, 324 pgs., $7.95.*
Volume III, Expedient Methods, *Chapter Two. ISBN 0-917512-26-X, 183 pgs., $7.95.*
Volume IV, A Parable, *Chapter Three. ISBN 0-917512-62-6, 371 pgs., $8.95.*
Volume V, Belief and Understanding, *Chapter Four. ISBN 0-917512-64- ISBN 0917-512-64-2, 200 pgs., $6.95.*
Volume VI, Medicinal Herbs, *Chapter Five, and* Conferring Predictions, *Chapter Six. ISBN 0-917512-65-0, 161 pgs., $6.95.*
Volume VII, Parable of the Transformation City, *Chapter Seven. ISBN 0-917512-93-6, 250 pgs., $7.95.*
Volume VIII, Five Hundred Disciples Receive Predictions, *Chapter Eight, and* Bestowing Predictions Upon Those Studying and Beyond Study, *Chapter Nine. ISBN 0-917512-71-5, 160 pgs., $6.95.*
Volume IX, Masters of the Dharma, *Chapter 10, and* Vision of the Jewelled Stupa, *Chapter 11. ISBN 0-917512-85-5, 270 pgs., $9.00.*

Volume X, Devadatta, *Chapter 12, and* Exhortation to Maintain, *Chapter 13.* ISBN 088139-34-0, 150 pgs., $5.00.
-*Further volumes forthcoming*-
Flower Adornment (Avatamsaka) Sutra- 大方廣佛華嚴經淺釋 *Known as the 'King of Kings' of all Buddhist scriptures because of its profundity and great length (81 rolls containing more than 700,000 Chinese characters). It contains the most complete explanation of the Buddha's state and the Bodhisattva's quest for Awakening. When completed the entire Sutra text with commentary is estimated to be from 75 to 100 volumes. The following volumes have been published to date:*
Verse Preface- 華嚴經疏序淺釋 *a succinct and eloquent verse commentary by T'ang Dynasty National Master Ch'ing Liang, who was the Master of seven emperors. The Preface gives a complete explanation of all the fundamental principles contained in the Sutra. This is the first English translation. Bi-lingual ed., Eng/Chin.* ISBN 0-917512-28-6, 244 pgs., $7.00.
Prologue- *a detailed explanation of the principles of the Sutra by National Master Ch'ing Liang, utilizing the Hsien Shou method of analysis known as the Ten Doors. Approx. 5-10 vols. upon completion. Following are volumes published to date:*
Volume One, *the First Door: Causes and Conditions of the Arisal of the Teaching.* ISBN 0-917512-66-9, 252 pgs., $10.00
Volume Two, *First part of the Second Door: the Stores and Teachings in Which It is Contained.* ISBN 0-917512-73-1, 230 pgs., $10.00.
Volume Three, *Explanation of the Second Door.* ISBN 0-917512-98-7, 220 pgs., $10.00.
Volume Four, *Completes the Second Door.* ISBN 0-88139-009-7, 170 pgs., $7.00. *Available Spring 1983.*
Flower Adorned Sea of Worlds, *Chapter 5, Part 1.* ISBN 0-917512-54-5, 250 pgs., $8.50.
Bright Enlightenment, *Chapter 9.* ISBN 0-88139-005-4, 225 pgs., $8.50.
Pure Conduct, *Chapter 11.* ISBN 0-917512-37-5, 255 pgs., $9.00.
Ten Dwellings, *Chapter 15.* ISBN 0-917512-77-4, 185 pgs., $8.00.
Brahma Conduct, *Chapter 16.* ISBN 0-917512-80-4, 65 pgs., $4.00.
The Merit and Virtue from First Bringing Forth the Mind, *Chapter 17.* ISBN 0-917512-83-9, 200 pgs., $7.00.
The Ten Inexhaustible Treasuries, *Chapter 22.* ISBN 0-917512-38-3, 184 pgs., $7.00.
Praises in the Tushita Heaven Palace, *Chapter 22.* ISBN 0-017512-39-1, 130 pgs., $5.00.
Ten Transferences, *Chapter 25, Part 1.* ISBN 0-917512-52-9, 250 pgs., $8.50. *Available Spring 1983.*
Ten Grounds, *Chapter 26, Part 1, First Ground of Happiness:* ISBN 917512-87-1, 234 pgs., $7.00; *Part 2, Second Ground of Leaving Filth and Third Ground of Emitting Light, and Fourth Ground of Blazing Wisdom:* ISBN 0-917512-74-X, 200 pgs., $8.00.
-*Further volumes forthcoming*-

Universal Worthy's Conduct, *Chapter 36.* ISBN 0-88139-011-9, 200 pgs., $7.50.
Entering the Dharma Realm, *Chapter 39. This chapter, which makes up one quarter of the entire Sutra, contains the spiritual journey of the Youth Good Wealth in his search for Ultimate Awakening. In his quest he meets fifty-three "Good Teachers," each of whom represents a successive stage on the Bodhisattva Path. This is the first*

English translation of this chapter. This work will be from 7-10 volumes when complete. Following volumes have been published to date:

Part One. Describes the setting for the youth's quest, and his meeting with Manjushri Bodhisattva. ISBN 0-917512-68-5, 280 pgs., $8.50.

Part Two. Good Wealth meets his first ten teachers, who represent the positions of the Ten Dwellings. ISBN 0-917512-70-7, 250 pgs., $8.50.

Part Three. Good Wealth is taught by the ten teachers who correspond to the Ten Conducts. ISBN 0-917512-73-1, 250 pgs., $8.50.

Part Four. Good Wealth meets the ten teachers who represent the Bodhisattvas of the Ten Transferences. ISBN 0-917512-76-6, 185 pgs., $8.00.

Part Five. Good Wealth meets the six teachers who represent the first six Grounds. ISBN 0-917512-81-2, 300 pgs., $9.00.

Part Six. Good Wealth meets the teachers on the seventh through tenth Grounds. ISBN 0-917512-48-0, 320 pgs., $9.00.

-further volumes forthcoming-

Universal Worthy's Conduct and Vows, *Chapter 40.* ISBN 0-917512-84-7, 300 pgs., $10.00.

Heart Sutra and Verses Without a Stand- *Probably the most popular Sutra in the world today, recited daily in most monasteries. Explains the meaning of prajna-paramita, the perfection of wisdom, which is able to clearly perceive the emptiness of all phenomena. Each line of text is accompanied by an eloquent verse by the Venerable Master Hsüan Hua, and his commentary contains an explanation of most of the fundamental Buddhist concepts.* ISBN 0-917512-28-7, 160 pgs., $7.50.

Shurangama Sutra-*The most detailed explanation of the Buddha's teachings concerning the mind. Includes an analysis of the location of the mind, an explanation of the origin of the cosmos, the specific workings of karma, the realms of existence, and the fifty kinds of deviant samadhi-concentrations which can delude us in our search for awakening. Also, twenty-five enlightened sages explain the methods they used to become enlightened. Entire eight-volume set at discount price of $65.00.*

Volume One, *Location of the mind; roots of the false and the true.* ISBN 0-917512-17-0, 289 pgs., $8.50.

Volume Two, *Individual and collective karma; revelation of the true mind through display of ten different aspects of seeing-nature.* ISBN 0-917512-25-1, 212 pgs., $8.50.

Volume Three, *Qualities of the sense-fields, their respective consciousnesses, and all the internal elemental forces of the universe. Explained as ultimately unreal, existing neither through causes nor arising spontaneously.* ISBN 0-917512-94-4, 240 pgs., $8.50.

Volume Four, *The formation of the world, the coming into being of sentient creatures, and the cycle of karmic retribution.* ISBN 0-917512-90-1, 200 pgs., $8.50.

Volume Five, *Twenty-five sages explain the method they used to transcend the realm of birth and death. "Returning the hearing to listen to the self-nature" selected as most appropriate for people in our world system.* ISBN 0-917512-91-X, 250 pgs., $8.50.

Volume Six, *The four clear and unalterable instructions on purity, how to establish a Bodhimanda, the wondrous functions of the Shur-*

angama Mantra, and the twelve categories of living beings.
ISBN 0-917512-97-9, 200 pgs., $8.50.

Volume Seven, *The fifty-five stages of the Bodhisattva's Path to Enlightenment, how beings fall into the hells, all the realms of existence of the ghosts, animals, people, immortals, and the various heavens.* ISBN 0-917512-97-9, 270 pgs., $8.50.

Volume Eight, *The fifty skandha-demon states, which cultivators get stuck in.* ISBN 917-512-35-9, 256 pgs., $8.50. Available Spring 1983.

Sixth Patriarch Sutra- *One of the foremost scriptures in Ch'an (Zen) Buddhism, describes the life and teachings of the remarkable Patriarch of the T'ang Dynasty, Great Master Hui Neng, who, though unable to read or write, was enlightened to the true nature of all things.* ISBN 0-917512-19-7, 235 pgs., $10.00. (Hardcover, $15.00).

Sutra in 42 Sections- *First Sutra to be transported from India and translated into Chinese in which the Buddha gives the most essential instructions for cultivating the Dharma, emphasizing renunciation, contentment, and patience.* ISBN 0-917512-15-4, 114 pgs., $4.00.

Sutra of the Past Vows of Earth Store Bodhisattva- *How Earth Store Bodhisattva became one of the greatest Bodhisattvas, foremost in vows. Explains the workings of karma, rebirth, and the various kinds of hells. First English translation. Hardcover only,* ISBN 0-917512-09-X, 235 pgs., $16.00. *English text without commentary for recitation,* ISBN 0-88139-502-1, 120 pgs., $6.00.

Vajra Prajna Paramita (Diamond) Sutra- *One of the most popular scriptures. Explains how the Bodhisattva relies on the perfection of wisdom to teach and transform beings.* ISBN 0-917512-02-2, 192 pgs., $8.00.

COMMENTARIAL LITERATURE:

Buddha Root Farm- *A collection of lectures explaining the practice and philosophy of the Pure Land School. Complete instructions; especially useful for beginners.* ISBN 0-917-512-08-1, 72 pgs., $4.00.

Cherishing Life- *Verses and brush drawings on not taking life, along with public records by Dharma Masters on cause and effect drawn from actual events and from people's memories of past lives as animals and their awareness of the reason for their retribution. For elementary age children as well as adults.* ISBN 0-88139-004-6, 150 pgs., $7.00.

City of 10,000 Buddhas Recitation Handbook-
Bi-lingual, Chinese/English. 240 pgs., $6.00. (2nd edition)

Great Compassion Dharma Transmission Verses of the Forty-two Hands and Eyes- *42 b/w photos of the Ven. Master Hua's self-portrait paintings of the 42 Hands and Eyes, and 42 b/w photos of copper reliefs of the 42 Hands and Eyes, with verses in Chinese (w/English translation) by the Venerable Master for each one.* ISBN 0-88139-002-X, 100 pgs., $16.00.

Human Roots- *Buddhist Stories for Young Readers. 14 stories from Buddhist Canon and hist. records.* ISBN 088139-500-S, 95 pgs., $4.00.

Herein Lies the Treasure-trove, *Vol. 1. Instructional talks of the Venerable Master at the City of 10,000 Buddhas during the last few years.* ISBN 0-88139-001-1, 250 pgs., $8.50.

Life-pulse of Loyalty and Reciprocity. *Instructions on not killing, the detrimental karmic effects of eating meat, and stories of reincarnation concerning these. For high school students, as well as adults. ISBN 0-88139-006-2, 250 pgs., $8.50.*

Listen to Yourself, Think It Over-*Instructions on practice of reciting the name of Kuan Yin Bodhisattva and how to cultivate Ch'an meditation. All instructions given during actual sessions. ISBN 0-917512-24-3, 153 pgs., $7.00.*

Pure Land and Ch'an Dharma Talks- *Instructions given during an Amitabha Buddha Recitation and Ch'an Meditation session. ISBN 0-917512-08-1, 72 pgs., $4.00.*

Shastra on the Door to Understanding the Hundred Dharmas. *Abhidharma text with commentary. ISBN 88139-003-8, 130 pgs., $6.50.*

Shurangama Mantra Commentary- 楞嚴咒疏句偈解 *An ancient text on how to practice the foremost mantra in the Buddha's teaching, including a line-by-line analysis of the Mantra. Vol. 1: 296 pgs, $8.50; Vol. 2: ISBN 0-917512-82-0, 200 pgs., $7.50; Vol. 3: ISBN 0-917512-36-7, 156 pgs., $6.50. All volumes in English and Chinese, Further Volumes forthcoming.*

Song of Enlightenment-*Famous lyric poem of the state of the Ch'an Sage, by the Venerable Master Yung Chia of the T'ang Dynasty. Available Spring 1983.*

The Ten Dharma Realms are not Beyond a Single Thought- *Eloquent poem on all the realms of being, accompanied by extensive commentarial material and drawings. ISBN 0-917512-12-X, 72 pgs., $4.00.*

Water-Mirror Reflecting Heaven- *Essay on the fundamental principle of cause and effect, with biographical material on contemporary Buddhist cultivation in China. ISBN 0-88139-501-3, 82 pgs., $4.00.*

BIOGRAPHICAL:

Records of the Life of the Venerable Master Hsüan Hua- *Life and teachings of the Venerable Master from his birthplace in China to the present time in America:*
Volume One, *ISBN 0-917512-07-3, 96 pgs., $5.00. (Spanish, $8.00.)*
Volume Two, *ISBN 0-917512-10-3, 229 pgs., $8.00.*
   -Further volumes forthcoming-

Pictorial Biography of the Venerable Master Hsü Yün. *Brush drawings to accompany prose and verses written by the Venerable Master Hua documenting Venerable Hsü Yün's life. Two-volume set, 104 sections of prose, verses and drawings. Vol. 1. ISBN 88139-008-9, 120 pgs., $7.00. Available Spring 1983.*

With One Heart Bowing to the City of 10,000 Buddhas- *Moving journals of American Bhikshus Heng Sure and Ch'au's pilgrimage from Gold Wheel Temple in Los Angeles to the City of 10,000 Buddhas, from May 1977 to October 1979.*
Volume One, *May 6-June 30, 1977. ISBN 0-917512-21-9, 180 pgs., $6.00*
Volume Two, *July 1-October 30, 1977. ISBN 0-917512-23-5, 322 pgs., $7*
Volume Three, *Oct. 30-Dec. 20, 1977. ISBN 0-917512-89-8, 154 pgs., $5*
Volume Four, *Dec. 17-Jan. 21, 1978. ISBN 0-917512-90-1, 136 pgs., $4*
Volume Five, *Jan. 28-Feb 18, 1978, ISBN 0-917512-91-X, 127 pgs., $4*
Volume Six, *Feb. 19-April 2, 1978, ISBN 0-917512-92-8, 200 pgs., $6*
Volume Seven, *Apr. 3- May 24, 1978. ISBN 0-917512-99-5, 160 pgs., $5*
Volume Eight, *May 24-Sept. 1978. ISBN 0-917512-53-7. 232 pgs., $7.50*

   -Further volumes forthcoming-

中文佛書目錄

中美佛教總會法界大學出版

經典部分：

① 大方廣佛華嚴經序淺釋（漢英對照）　美國萬佛城宣化上人講解，全一冊。定價美金七元。

② 大方廣佛華嚴經疏淺釋（平裝四冊）　美國萬佛城宣化上人講解。

第一冊（第一門，教起因緣）定價美金五元。

第二冊（第二門，藏教所攝）定價美金八元五角。

第三冊（第三門，義理分齊）定價美金八元五角。

第四冊（第七門，部類品會。第八門，傳譯感通。第九門，總譯名題。第十門，別解文義）定價美金五元

③ 大方廣佛華嚴經淺釋（平裝八冊）　美國萬佛城宣化上人講解。

第一冊（世主妙嚴品第一，卷一至卷二）定價美金七元。

第二冊（世主妙嚴品第一，卷三）定價美金五元。

第三冊（世主妙嚴品第一，卷四至卷五）定價美金七元。

第四冊（如來現相品第二。普賢三昧品第三。世界成就品第四）定價美金五元。

第五冊（華藏世界品第五。毘盧遮那品第六。如來名號品第七。四聖諦品第八）定價美金七元。

第六冊（光明覺品第九。菩薩問明品第十。淨行品第十一）定價美金七元。

第七冊（賢首品第十二。升須彌山頂品第十三。須彌頂山偈讚第十四。十住品第十五）定價美金七元

第八冊（梵行品第十六。初發心功德品第十七。明法品第十八。升夜摩天品第十九。夜摩偈讚品第二十）定價美金五元。

佛書部分：

① 永嘉大師證道歌詮釋（全一冊） 美國萬佛城宣化上人講解 定價美金二元五角。
② 緇門崇行錄 蓮池大師著 弘一大師集 （贈閱）
③ 宣化上人偈讚闡釋錄（全一冊） （贈閱）
④ 宣化禪師事蹟（全一冊） 定價美金五元
⑤ 放眼觀世界（亞洲弘法記）（全一冊） 定價美金四元。
⑥ 修行者的消息（三步一拜兩行者一心頂禮萬佛城之來鴻） （贈閱）
⑦ 佛教精進者的日記（平裝上冊） 定價美金六元
⑧ 萬佛城雜誌月刊（漢英合刊） 定價一年美金二十二元。三年美金六十元。

即將出版：

① 大方廣佛華嚴經淺釋（十定品至入法界品）
② 楞嚴咒疏句偈解（漢英對照）（第二冊）
③ 梵網經講錄（漢英對照）（下冊）
④ 地藏菩薩本願經淺釋
⑤ 大佛頂首楞嚴經淺釋
⑥ 沙彌律儀淺釋
⑦ 佛教精進者的日記（下冊）
⑧ 宣化上人語錄
⑨ 萬佛城聯語集

總流通處：中美佛教總會金山寺

Gold mt. Monastery 1731 15th St. San Francisco, CA.94103 U.S.A.

④大方廣佛華嚴經十地品淺釋（平裝三冊）美國萬佛城宣化上人講解。
第一冊（第一歡喜地）（漢英對照）定價美金七元。
第二冊（第二離垢地。第三發光地。第四燄慧地。第五難勝地）定價美金五元。
第三冊（第六現前地。第七遠行地。第八不動地。第九善慧地。第十法雲地）定價美金六元。

⑤千手千眼大悲心陀羅尼經（全一冊）定價美金六元。

⑥般若波羅蜜多心經非台頌解（全一冊）美國萬佛城宣化上人講解 定價美金五元。

⑦楞嚴咒疏句偈解（漢英對照）（第一冊）美國萬佛城宣化上人講解 定價美金八元五角。

⑧梵網經講錄（漢英對照）（上冊）慧僧法師述 定價美金十元。

南無阿彌陀佛

南無觀世音菩薩

南無大勢至菩薩

聖作行意教
三其奉其佛
方惡善淨諸
諸眾自是
西

Dharma Protector Wei T'o Bodhisattva

Verse of Transference

May the merit and virtue accrued from this work,
Adorn the Buddhas' Pure Lands,
Repaying four kinds of kindness above,
And aiding those suffering in the paths below.

May those who see and hear of this.
All bring forth the resolve for Bodhi,
And when this retribution body is over,
Be born together in ultimate bliss.